Hodder

SWIMMING

Helen Elkington,
Jane Chamberlain ~ Roberta Hatt

COLLEGE OF RIPON
AND YORK ST JOHN
LIBRARY

1

2

Hodder & Stoughton

British Library Cataloguing in Publication Data

A Catalogue entry for this title is available from the British Library

ISBN 0 340 68353 8

First published 1998
Impression number   10 9 8 7 6 5 4 3 2 1
Year   2000 1999 1998

Typeset by Fakenham Photosetting Ltd, Fakenham, Norfolk.
Printed in Great Britain for Hodder & Stoughton Educational, a division of Hodder Headline Plc, 339 Euston Road, London NW1 3BH by Scotprint Ltd, Musselburgh, Scotland

Contents

Introduction   **1**

   The safety aspect   1
   The value of swimming   1
   The teacher's philosophy   3
   The aims of swimming   3

PART I
SWIMMING AND EDUCATIONAL THEORY

Chapter 1   **Pupil and teacher characteristics**   **7**

   Individual differences between pupils   7
   Teacher qualities   10

Chapter 2   **The analysis and assessment of swimming** **12**

   Analysis   12
   Assessment   14

Chapter 3   **Learning and motivation**   **18**

   Principles of learning through being rewarded   18
   Principles of learning through understanding   20
   Motivation and needs   22

Chapter 4   **Group work**   **25**

   Styles and strategies to cope with individual differences 26

PART II
THE PRACTICE OF SWIMMING

Chapter 5   **Setting the scene**   **35**

   Pool safety and hygiene   35
   Equipment   35
   The environment   38

Chapter 6   **Early lessons and fundamentals**   **39**

               Introducing children to water   39
               The first stage   40
               The second stage   43
               Game activities   44
               Fundamentals   46
               Watermanship   48

Chapter 7   **Strokes**   **51**

               The back crawl stroke   51
               The front crawl stroke   59
               The breaststroke   68
               The inverted breaststroke   75
               The dolphin butterfly stroke   78

Chapter 8   **General stroke analysis**   **86**

               Stroke counting   89

Chapter 9   **Breathing**   **96**

               Exhalation and inhalation   96
               Method of breathing   96
               Teaching breathing   98

Chapter 10   **Starts and turns**   **101**

               Racing starts from the poolside or starting block   101
               The back-crawl start   103
               Teaching the start   104
               Turning   107

Chapter 11   **Diving**   **114**

               Shallow-end activities   114
               The sitting dive   116
               The kneeling dive   116
               The lunge dive   117
               The crouch dive   117
               The plunge dive   117
               The plain header   118

Chapter 12   **Water safety**   **121**

               Safety and discipline   121

Hygiene   122
The Water Safety Code   123
Entries   125

Chapter 13   **Lesson planning**   **129**

Units of work and lesson preparation   129
Lesson planning   130
Lesson organisation   131
Lesson evaluation   133
Sample lesson plans   142

Appendix I   **Glossary of terms**   **149**

Appendix II   **Analogies for the teacher of swimming**   **150**

Index   **154**

Introduction

THE SAFETY ASPECT

'Swimming is an essential part of every child's physical education.'

This view, expressed by Helen Elkington (1978), has always been accepted by a number of teachers of Physical Education. Increasingly, the essential need for all young people to be able to cope with the environment of water in order at least to be able to save their own lives has been recognised, and in addition, a basic skill in swimming is a prerequisite for a wider range of enjoyable and valuable water-based activities, such as sailing, canoeing or water skiing.

Since the Dearing Review of the National Curriculum (1994), swimming has been given additional priority in the revised National Curriculum for Physical Education. It is seen as an essential life skill. However, the stipulated requirement for pupils to swim 25 metres must be treated with a good deal of caution. The pupil may feel confident and then get into a situation where they are out of their depth. Teachers *must* ensure that all pupils are *totally* confident in water by being able to float and swim both on the surface and underwater for much further than just 25 metres. This may of course require swimming to be taught beyond Key Stage 2, although economic and practical difficulties involved in this requirement need to be recognised.

THE VALUE OF SWIMMING

It is our belief that swimming is not only a fundamental life skill but equally importantly a skill which provides young people with the opportunity to develop their intellectual, social and emotional skills. If, as the revised National Curriculum for Physical Education (PE) requires, pupils should acquire healthy lifestyles and positive attitudes, then swimming should be part of the programme which will encourage self-confidence, reliance, independence and judgement.

Swimming can offer children with disabilities enjoyable opportunities for success, higher social status and boosted confidence. The support of the water, the non-stressful environment, can give children with severe disabilities the confidence and the freedom they need in order to exercise the whole body. Swimming is also a sport which can readily be introduced to people of all ethnic backgrounds. Groups of Moslem girls can be introduced to swimming as a self-contained group, able to wear the required clothing and thus undertake a healthy life style.

The immense value of swimming lies in its contribution to survival, health and fitness, and fun. The new PE curriculum now recognises to some extent the importance of these issues.

Survival

Everyone should be given the opportunity to become a competent swimmer. Water is a tempting and enjoyable environment, but is also a dangerous one which must be respected. Too many children are classified as swimmers when they have merely struggled down the length of a pool. This is only a beginning. They must be enabled to improve their technique, stamina and strength, and to be able to orientate themselves in water in more taxing circumstances and for considerably greater distances. Children need to learn how to survive. The teacher must ensure that the pupils are aware of safety and of their own limitations. Should they put themselves in danger either in a swimming pool or in any water outside, then they must be aware of the potential danger they may be causing to a rescuer. Details of the Water Safety Code are provided in Chapter 1. Much of this teaching forms an element of important social education: it can develop social awareness in young people and sensitise them to the needs of others and of the community.

Health and fitness

Not without justification, swimming is an extremely popular form of exercise, for both able-bodied and disabled people. It uses all the muscles of the body, it exercises the cardio-vascular system, and, when undertaken in a regular pattern, can burn off fat and increase and develop muscle fibres. Muscles are toned and strength and stamina are increased, and the individual is then more able to cope with the demands of everyday life and to rise to any extra demands which may suddenly be placed on the body. Age is no barrier; it is as suitable for individuals (in a safe pool environment) as it is for groups; and it is an ideal family activity. Swimming is an unusual and unique sport in that the water supports the body so providing opportunity for non-stressful exercise.

Young people who are made aware of these values may become intellectually more understanding of their own bodies, and begin to have a social awareness of a healthy lifestyle.

Fun

Swimming can start to be fun from the moment a learner has their feet off the bottom of the pool. All kinds of watersports and activities become possible, with a vast number of physical and social advantages, if introduced in an imaginative way. Having fun also depends on the role of the teacher, and more thought will be given to this in Chapter 1. The sport needs to be introduced in an irresistible way. The environment must be conducive to learning: warm, with sufficient space for each pupil and adequate swimming aids. The teacher may need to adapt the environment in order to ensure that the pupils feel safe, secure and at ease. If the pool is not sloped and is too deep, then ropes can be installed to ensure the pupils have a secure hold. Further points on this matter will be considered in Chapter 3. Every child must experience success in a lesson, no matter how small a step this might be.

THE TEACHER'S PHILOSOPHY

Each and every teacher has, if not explicitly, then implicitly, a philosophy of education. If, as one would hope, every teacher is a truly reflective professional, then it is appropriate for each teacher to think through and develop their own philosophy of education, with an awareness of its methods and techniques, and its strengths and limitations. This will then enable them to provide the written and verbal evidence that the Ofsted inspectors are seeking. To this end, a variety of different views and theories on the nature of education will be considered, with illustrations from the teaching of swimming. It is hoped that individual primary teachers will then make their choice of methods and techniques according to their own beliefs and be able to justify them.

THE AIMS OF SWIMMING

Education generally, and the teaching of swimming likewise, is value-laden. Individual teachers have both values and (as already indicated) a philosophy of eduction, be it only implicit, which leads to every teacher having aims for their classes which hopefully will become more clearly articulated as the teacher becomes more knowledgeable and proficient. Views generally on the nature and purposes of education vary considerably. Some would argue that pupils are empty vessels waiting to be filled with information which needs to be absorbed and regurgitated at the appropriate times. This view leads to pupils being controlled and conditioned, instructed and commanded. Others would argue that pupils are active creative individuals wanting to make sense of their environment. This leads to pupils being allowed to discover for themselves, to be active in their learning, the teacher here being a guide, an instigator of learning.

The Education Reform Act (1988) itself includes a statement of aims, and each school is likewise required to have a statement of its own aims clearly set out for the parents. The teacher of swimming will need to be operating within these broad guidelines whilst also having the independence to clearly state their own. Many of the current textbooks on swimming teaching have dealt with the techniques and skills of the strokes and allied activities. It is our belief that the teacher of swimming can only be fully effective if they know and understand *why* a certain procedure is recommended. To this end, a section of the book has been written which attempts to draw on teaching/learning theory in order to justify certain recommendations and to deepen the teacher's knowledge and understanding both of the individual natures of their pupils and of how each human being learns most effectively, hopefully then helping to clarify aims and philosophy. Direct links will be made between the underlying theory and the practice of teaching swimming.

Hodder Primary PE: Swimming is designed to further the understanding of both students and existing teachers of swimming who wish to both begin and update their knowledge and experience. In looking at different stages of child development as well as teaching/learning theory, our aim is to provide all teachers of swimming at Key Stages 1 and 2 with the knowledge they will require to make their lessons challenging, enjoyable and effective.

Note: throughout the text, 'they' is used to refer to 'he' or 'she'.

SWIMMING
AND
EDUCATIONAL THEORY

Pupil and teacher characteristics

There are very few children who for medical reasons are unable to participate in swimming, and it is also an activity in which boys and girls from whatever cultural group can take part. This not to say, however, that there are no individual differences. There are, and the teacher needs to be aware of their nature and deal with them sensitively by adopting different strategies (suggestions for some are made in Chapter 4). There will be differences in physical development, intelligence, and social and cultural background, all of which will affect the different pupils' responses to swimming.

Physical differences

The Key Stage 2 period is a stage of both consolidation and rapid growth for pupils. Account must be taken of the age and experience of the pupil when deciding what are their precise physical needs, and a basic understanding of the pupils' physical capabilities is required. Teachers need to take account of the pupils' nutrition and possible lack of exercise when tasks are being devised. The youngster coming to school having had no breakfast will not have much stamina or energy in a lesson at the end of a morning, and pupils fasting through Ramadan will be similarly affected. Many pupils these days are driven to school and spend most of their leisure time in sedentary activities in the home. This means that pupils may have little kinaesthetic knowledge, i.e. a limited feel for movement. To gain a sense of body awareness, physical movement needs to be frequently practised, and children here need to set their own challenges. Opportunities for children to play even in the street, let alone in the open countryside, have been considerably reduced in recent years, and this means that the teacher of Physical Education can no longer rely on certain elementary movement skills having been learned, and must therefore start at a much more basic level and introduce work on simpler and less challenging skills: prior to the first school lesson in the swimming pool, a pupil may have had no experience of being in such an environment. Body composition and structure – including the amount of body fat, and flexibility of the joints – will also influence the pupil's ability to perform the correct technique.

Children, of course, develop at vastly different rates, and these differences can dramatically affect confidence, self-esteem and the capacity for new learning. There is no place where physical development is more obvious than in the swimming pool, and the teacher needs to be sensitive to the needs and susceptibilities of their pupils in this respect. The early developer, entering puberty before the vast majority of the class, may wish either to avoid the swimming lesson or to show off, depending on their sex. In any case, when nearing puberty, the rates of physical development of boys and girls are very different and lead to very different skeletal and muscular structures, and for this reason the teacher will need to set tasks such that all are appropriately stretched and challenged. (Suggestions are made in Chapter 4.)

Intellectual differences

Most psychologists agree that some form or degree of interaction between heredity and the environment takes place in the development of intelligence. Even in swimming lessons, difference in intellectual ability may influence the pupils' performance, and Ofsted inspectors are now looking for teachers to differentiate both by task and by outcome in all lessons, according to individual ability. The teacher will need to group pupils with the least ability in the shallow end of a graduated pool, and tasks set, the language used, and the illustrations given to explain tasks, will all need to be geared to the pupil's level of understanding. All the more reason, then, that the term 'intelligence' should be fully understood. Teachers should make sure that they do not use this term – or associated terms such as 'dull', 'stupid' or 'bright' for example – ill-advisedly. Work undertaken by sociologists on the labelling process show just how powerful the effect of such terms can be. A label given and used by an influential and significant other person such as a teacher will be accepted and lived up to. Telling a pupil they are capable will boost confidence, but telling the pupil they are hopeless or incapable will have the reverse effect.

One further very important attribute of swimming is that it can encourage children to draw on previous learning, skills and abilities and then apply these to the task of stroke improvement. The chapters on the principles by which pupils learn, as well as the chapters on strokes, will give illustrations of the ways in which previous experience can aid the technique of strokes. In the light of what has just been said, teachers need to be very sensitive to the judgements they apply to their pupils' behaviour and performance.

Not only are there differences both in pupils' innate intellectual ability and in the environment which either encourages or hinders its development, but we have also been shown by Jean Piaget that children think in very different ways from adults. His ideas on the progression and development of thinking in children and adolescents need careful scrutiny. If Piaget is right and children between the ages of 8 and 11 think in very concrete terms, then the greater the number of *illustrations* given to pupils of these ages, the better. When teaching the doggy paddle, tell the child to reach for the end of the nose like an Alsatian, take hold of a goldfish and put it in the bowl behind them. When teaching a supine position, let them imagine supporting a plate of food on the tummy; make the arm slice through butter in the arm entry in the backstroke. Many such illustrations may help the younger and less able pupil to understand the body position required for correct technique.

Social and cultural differences

No student comes to a lesson totally as an individual. All are members of other social groups gender-based, social-class-based, or with a specific ethnicity – and the values, attitudes and patterns of behaviour involved here are all different. All of these specific subcultures have a profound impact on the pupils' attitudes to swimming. Much has been written by sociologists on the nature and influence of culture and subculture. On the one hand, family background has been shown to be powerfully influential in educational achievement and in attitudes to education. However, other studies have shown how schools can in fact compensate for deficiencies in home background, and further studies have shown how the playground culture has a unique and particular way of coping with school life. The work of Vygotsky has shown how important adults are in structuring children's understanding. Vygotsky shows how the language and forms of behaviour found in their culture help to develop pupils' cognitive skills and strategies. Furthermore, there is a good deal of research which explores many differences in attitudes and involvement in sport generally between boys and girls.

There is a need, therefore, for the teacher to be aware of the variety of groups to which pupils belong and to consider which values, attitudes and patterns of behaviour pertain to them. Pupils from middle-class homes may have different values, attitudes and experiences in relation to swimming from those from working-class homes; and the same may be true of those from different ethnic homes. Differences in child-rearing practices in different homes, and their impact on education have been explored extensively, and a good deal of work has also been undertaken on social and cultural influences on women in sport. (In 1990, of the women who participated in sport, 13% took part in swimming, the third highest percentage.) The teacher needs to be sensitive to all the differences and in certain circumstances modify or adapt their above-mentioned teaching style to take account of these differences (see Chapter 5). Pupils will have seen different role models in their home and community: the pupil who is taken to a community pool and sees mother or father swimming, will have a different mental set from the pupil who has never witnessed any activity in water. Even if their technique is not correct, the former pupil will already have become accustomed to the environment and will know what it feels like to propel oneself through the water. On the other hand, parents' fear of water may be conveyed subconsciously to another child.

Language is the medium of thinking and learning. A pupil whose first language is not English may well have difficulty with the technical terms applied in swimming, and analogies used by the teacher to explain technique need to take account of the pupil's home experiences. (See Appendix II.)

TEACHER QUALITIES

At a conference held by Ofsted, SCAA and the Teacher Training Agency, there was general agreement on a number of characteristics which were deemed to make an effective teacher. Amongst these were:

- an understanding of what pupils can and need to learn
- the ability to ask effective questions
- to ensure appropriate pace
- a sense of humour
- commitment to and enthusiasm for the job
- clarity in communication
- an ability to motivate pupils to learn
- an ability to be self-critical and to reflect on their teaching.

All of these characteristics apply to the teacher of swimming. The argument presented throughout this text is that of the importance of the role of the teacher as a motivator and instigator of learning. A key factor in this role is that of *teacher presentation*. Above all, the teacher of swimming needs to be dynamic and enthusiastic. A swimming pool is often a difficult environment in which to teach since acoustics can be poor. The teacher's voice is therefore a vital instrument. The teacher needs to be able to throw their voice to the end of the pool *without strain*, and for this reason their breathing *must* come from the diaphragm. As with all teaching, pitch, volume and tone must be varied so as to gain attention and maintain concentration. The tone of voice can indicate enthusiasm, pleasure – indeed, all the emotions – and pupils can be inspired by the way in which the voice is used. Diction also needs to be very clear. Certain words at times need to be overemphasised in order to stress the important part of an exercise – e.g. '*push* and glide'. Words may need extra enunciation so that pupils can lip-read directions. Keep sentences short and pertinent, giving only essential information and do avoid crouching down to speak to those in the pool.

In some pool environments, it is virtually impossible to speak clearly, so the teacher then needs to be able to act and to mime. Allied to teacher presentation and the use of voice is therefore the use of *demonstration*. The teacher can be seen as a role model, so although they will not be in the water with the pupils, they must be able to demonstrate from the bathside accurately and efficiently. Thought must be given to the position of the teacher on the poolside so that all can see, and then the attention of the pupils needs to be carefully focused (see the work on attention and perception in Chapter 3). The whole body must be involved in showing what is expected, be it the technique of arm or legs or positioning in the pool. The angle demonstrated must be as near to the swimming position as possible, and so may need a good deal of practise in front of a mirror to perfect. If a pupil is demonstrating, the same principles apply. This may mean that the others in the class will need to come out of the water in order to see the demonstrator from the required position. If, for example, pupils need to observe the depth of the leg action, then the observers need to be on the poolside. The teacher must be positioned so that all those on the poolside plus the demonstrator can be seen clearly. Teachers should use the whistle very sparingly   only in emergency situations.

The analysis and assessment of swimming

Skill analysis depends on acute observation and a knowledge of correct technique. A knowledge of anatomy as well as some understanding of physical forces will all deepen the teacher's ability to coach and improve upon pupils' performances. Whilst this knowledge will broaden and deepen the teacher's ability to coach and teach, care must be taken to make sure that instructions given to the pupils to enable them to improve must be within their own experience and understanding. (See Chapters 1 and 3.)

Children's acquisition of skill depends on the abilities of the child, the nature of the task and the environment within which it is situated. The latter two factors are within the control of the teacher to a certain degree, but an understanding of the former is also required for sensitive teaching. At birth, the human infant possesses both reflex movements and spontaneous movements. Both of these kinds of movement can be seen in the infant from a very early age when placed in water. The earlier the infant begins to experience movement in and through water in a supportive environment, the better these instinctive 'swimming' actions will develop.

> There is an argument which states that by the age of 7 a child will have acquired all of the naturally developing skills s/he will ever possess. Between 7 and puberty a child starts to refine the movements by playing with them in different contexts.
>
> (D. A. Sugden in J. Whitehead (ed) 1993)

A variable number of pupils will have had the experience of being taken to a pool as a baby and so for some pupils the primary teacher will be providing the initial experiences. (See Chapter 1 for further thoughts on individual differences.) The teacher needs to provide opportunities both for the early exploration of water and for the refinement of earlier acquired skills. The pupil must be able to understand clearly the skill they are required to learn, as well as *why* it is to be learned. Although the need to *practise* skills will be emphasised, *meaningless* practices are of course demotivating. The teacher needs to refer to the ideas written on the nature of pupils' learning in Chapter 2.

Prior to starting to teach, the teacher needs to give thought to the number of pupils in their care. Safety rules will be set by the pool authority and/or Local Education Authority. The teacher must know these rules, as well as the maximum number of pupils allowed in the particular pool, and the most appropriate number will depend on the age and ability of the pupils. No teacher, however capable, can teach over-large numbers – instead they will be merely occupied. This is not good enough: the pupils must be *taught* in each and every lesson. The style and philosophy will vary, but each pupil should improve skill acquisition in each lesson.

In order for this to happen, the teacher must know the required progressions for each stroke. Then the teacher will need to train their observation of pupils' performances so to identify weaknesses, understand their causes and know how to rectify them. There is a crucial need for teaching points to be given to the pupils at each and every stage of the lesson. It is not adequate merely for a global task to be set, such as a number of lengths to be swum. The appropriate specific teaching point must also always be given – for example, 'Swim three lengths of the pool thinking about the position of the hand as it enters the water.' It may be possible to group the pupils according to ability and then set a task which tests the number of widths swum in a particular number of minutes rather than telling all to swim two widths since this task will then be completed at different times. If all are swimming for a set number of minutes, then the teacher can walk along the side of the pool observing and coaching. Alternatively, the teacher may give the class one crucial teaching point to think about and work on until this has been mastered. The class can be told to stop for breath when needed and then keep going. Whilst the class is practising, the teacher again coaches individuals. Further reference is made to this recommendation in Chapter 4.

Tasks and guidance

Two kinds of tasks might be set: *objective* and *subjective*. An objective task is one which concentrates on an objective measure – for example, 'See how many lengths can be swum in two minutes', 'Can you swim three lengths without stopping?' In this form of task, style and technique are not the important criteria. A subjective task, however, is one which does concentrate on style and technique – for example, 'Swim for two minutes on the back, making sure the arms move like a windmill.'

The teacher may then think in terms of there being three forms of guidance, each of which has a value at an appropriate time:

1 A *visual* form of guidance may be provided by either the teacher or a pupil. A visual demonstration may be used to teach a new aspect of a stroke, or for encouragement.

2 *Verbal guidance* is likely to be provided by the teacher, though thought needs to be given to the need to question the pupils about their performance. This serves to focus attention, to ensure that they understand the purpose of the practice, and to maintain discipline and control. (A list of analogies for use in verbal instructions in lessons has been provided at the end of the text) (see pages 150–53).

3 *Manual guidance*, where the teacher manually places the pupils' limb/s in the correct position, also has an important place in teaching. It is a way of ensuring that the pupil acquires a *kinaesthetic* feel for movement. However, this is a form of guidance which must be used with great caution and sensitivity, probably as a last resort and always publicly.

ASSESSMENT

Having prepared lessons in detail in advance, the teacher will now have to assess the pupils' abilities and performances. Macintosh and Hale (1976) summarised what they considered to be the main purposes of assessment as follows:

● diagnosis
● evaluation
● guidance
● grading
● selection
● prediction.

The teacher of swimming needs to go through at least the first four of these criteria in class teaching. The latter two may be more relevant to the competitive swimmer, selecting for a team or competition and/or predicting future development in that field. If the class teaching of swimming is to improve, the teacher will need to diagnose errors, evaluate abilities and performance, guide the pupil towards improved performance, for the eventual purposes of recording and reporting, and making a grade.

The PE National Curriculum Key Stage 2 Programme of Study (Department for Education, 1995) requires that pupils '...should be taught...

> to swim unaided, competently and safely, for at least 25 metres; ... a variety of means of propulsion using either arms or legs or both, and how to develop effective an efficient swimming strokes on the front and the back;'

The End of Key Stage Descriptor (Department for Education, 1995) requires that

> 'they practise, improve and refine performance, and repeat series of movements they have performed previously, with increasing control and accuracy ... They make simple judgements about their own and others' performance, and use this information effectively to improve the accuracy, quality and variety of their own performance.'

These guidelines give little detailed instruction to the teacher on relative standards of performance to be expected at this age, and the teacher has to devise the assessment objectives for each aspect of the swimming curriculum. It is a government requirement for all state schools to report on each pupil's performance in the National Curriculum subjects at the end of each school year. The teacher then needs to devise objectives for each year of pupils and aspect of swimming which will enable that reporting to be both *developmental* or *formative* – and *summative*. – Formative assessment should be conveyed to the pupil during the year, for this is the form of assessment which should be used by both the teacher and the pupil to modify and improve performance as the lessons develop. Summative assessment is that which sums up all the achievements of the complete course and will certainly be conveyed on the annual report form.

Norm-based or criterion-based

Assessment may be *norm-based* or *criterion-based*. Much of the assessment in swimming involves the latter form, in which there is an objective criterion against which a swimmer is judged. In order to fulfil these tasks, style and technique are not of prime importance. A task here might be, for example, to assess the distance covered in a particular length of time. Following on from this are the objective practical tasks of the kind covered later. Norm-based assessment, on the other hand, requires pupils to be ranked in terms of their peers, be they those in the class with them or those in the year group nationally. This ranking against others might also be made in terms of success at meeting an objective criterion, so that, for example, the most able, graded

A, have swum 25 metres in 3 minutes. Or this ranking might be a subjective judgement made, for example, on the most efficiently performed backstroke. These in turn lead on to subjective practical tasks of the kind covered later in the book. However skilled a teacher is at observing and analysing technique, judgements made about style are bound, indeed, to be subjective.

Reliability and validity

There are two statistical criteria which should be taken into account in assessment procedures if these are to be adequate and credible: *reliability* and *validity*. A reliable assessment is one in which a pupil will gain the same score consistently on different occasions regardless of who is marking the test. A valid assessment is one which will genuinely test what it claims to test. It should sample the whole course, and may be used to predict future success. This is of course easier when an objective task has been set, but the teacher also needs to know in fine detail the elements which make up an efficient, technically accurate stroke so that they can identify precisely why a particular mark has been given. Thought needs to be given to the ideas raised in Chapter 3 on goal-setting as a method, with its consequent assessment. The suggestion is made there that personal development and improvement should be the criteria, recognising that many pupils of primary-school age are aiming for social approval rather than competitive achievement.

A good assessment should be practicable, comprehensive, dynamic and unobtrusive. The primary-school teacher might think about using limited resources carefully, have a simple programme where possible, cover the range of skills and techniques required, be ready to adapt to changing circumstances, and also try not to let the assessment interfere with class teaching.

Records and awards

Throughout swimming courses, performance should be assessed in terms of: distance covered; depth covered; time taken; stroke efficiency. The first three aspects can be assessed objectively. When assessing stroke efficiency, the teacher might use the acronym BLABT to remind them of those features of the stroke which need attention, namely: **B**ody position; **L**eg action; **A**rm action; **B**reathing; **T**iming. Each pupil will need to be assessed in each aspect of each stroke and a record kept of their technique and level of efficiency. Marks out of 10 might be given for BLABT, with the teacher being able to justify why marks have been taken away from 10 in each case. A stroke count over a measured distance might be taken, first at an average pace, then at a fast pace. An undue increase in the number of strokes would indicate an inefficient stroke as the pupil snatches at, rather than pulls, the water.

Many books and articles on the PE National Curriculum have provided advice and guidance on the format of records to be kept on pupils' progress. Some Local Education Authorities have stipulated the forms which should be used. Teachers must make their own judgements. Suffice it to say here that detailed and objective assessment needs to be kept to substantiate the subjective judgements being made, with both of these reported to pupils and parents.

It has also been suggested that pupils be assessed on improvement and effort rather than on performance and ability.

In the light of the above, careful thought is needed concerning the various award schemes on offer. It is possible for awards to determine the work which is being done in schools. On the other hand, there is the opinion that awards should serve only to recognise the work that has been achieved. The task group set up initially to look at assessment in the National Curriculum strongly believed that testing should not determine either the scheme of work or the individual lesson: the design of the curriculum should start with aims, then consider content and methods and finally result in assessment.

If validity and reliability are to be achieved in award schemes (as they should be), then careful thought needs to be given to the criteria for assessment. A scheme needs to clearly and unambiguously state what these criteria are, and the assessors then need to judge very carefully. An outside assessor needs at least to validate, if not to make, the award. Recognition has already been given to the grave dangers of allowing a pupil to think that they have achieved 25 metres swimming when this has not been done with any degree of skill or recognisable stroke.

Learning and motivation

PRINCIPLES OF LEARNING THROUGH BEING REWARDED

One of the most basic and early ways in which we learn is by being rewarded or *conditioned*. If we study the works of psychologists concerned with how we learn, we find the theory of Skinner (1953) which argues that learning and behaviour are synonymous. We have no way of accurately judging what takes place inside the brain, so the only evidence that learning has taken place is when certain forms of behaviour occur. This would seem to be a theory with which primary teachers are almost innately familiar, and it is one with which most would agree, and which would seem to be eminently appropriate for the teacher of swimming. At times, this behaviour is random, resulting from instinct, reflex actions and/or spontaneous movements. Much learning then starts as trial and error movements. If we then find a particular piece of behaviour satisfying or rewarding in some way, we repeat that behaviour. With satisfaction and a number of repetitions, the behaviour becomes firmly established. The teacher of swimming may start pupils off by allowing them to explore the water for themselves. A baby of a few months old reacts and responds in an innate, random way to exercise control over the water. This principle can also be explored with the older child. A primary-school child can be allowed to find the ways in which they feel most comfortable moving through the water. The teacher will then pick up on those movements which are appropriate for particular conventional strokes, and this can well result in a multi-stroke approach to the lesson.

The way to judge whether or not a pupil has learned a particular skill is by assessing the performance. Skinner's ideas with regard to reward, or *reinforcement*, are also valuable for the primary teacher to understand. According to Skinner, the teacher needs to reward the very slightest approximation towards the learning that is required. As the small progression of learning is established, the teacher then omits the reward until the next time that a further move towards the ultimate acquisition of the skill takes place. As the learning is repeated, the rewards given become less frequent and more irregular, until the pleasure in the performance for its own sake becomes the reward and the skill is permanently learnt. If the teacher also accepts Skinner's premise that all learning required should occur in very finely graded, small steps, then it is easy to ensure that the pupil gets frequent and satisfying reinforcement.

Each stroke in swimming can indeed be broken down into very finely graded steps. Some primary teachers may be familiar with the seemingly 'new' ideas in the Maths programme, entitled Kumin. In this programme, mathematical skills are ordered and ranked in very finely graded steps. The pupil then practises the skills many times in order to consolidate learning. The same principles need to apply to the basic strokes in swimming. Look at the fine progressions in the backstroke, for instance, in Chapter 7. These are very finely graded so that the challenge to the average learner is within their grasp with only a little effort. Once the new skill has been attained, then practice, practice and more practice is required to ensure that the movement is engrained in the cortex of the brain and the movement is learned. The primary-school pupil enjoys repetition of physical skills for its own sake. At times, however, repetition can become tiresome. The teacher must therefore be sensitive to the feelings of the pupil and be able to assess the development of the pupil's *learning curve* so to judge when to introduce a variety of practice. Thorndike's Laws of Exercise and of Effect are also relevant here. By the Law of Effect, Thorndike claims that a random response to a stimulus is reinforced if it is rewarding. Should it prove not to be rewarding, then an alternative response will be sought. His Law of Exercise argues that multiple repetitions of stimulus and response will ensure that a piece of behaviour is strengthened provided that knowledge of results also occurs. This means that the teacher should ensure not only a practice of behavioural responses but also that a pupil recognises that their performance is correct.

What is it that rewards the primary-school child? The success in swimming itself of course rewards, but most frequently it is praise from the teacher, who is still a powerful and influential figure in the life of most children of this age. So, praise the slightest improvement in the acquisition of skill. During each lesson, every child should have been praised for effort and achievement, and the teacher's tone of voice should ensure that the pupil realises that the 'Well done' is sincerely meant. The teacher's body language, too, must support the praise. Indeed, in an environment where it is difficult to convey verbal information, body language alone can convey pleasure and praise. Do not over-praise, however: praise or a reward, must be for genuine achievement, otherwise the teacher will be rewarding behaviour that is inappropriate and not required. There will then come a time when the reinforcement needs to be more concrete. Many pupils gain a feeling of achievement, which in itself is rewarding, from demonstrating to their peers, and even the weakest swimmer can demonstrate something. If the class has been grouped into a number of ability groups, then at least one pupil from each group can be selected to demonstrate. The most basic achievement can be shown to peers and so used as a reward. Later, a tangible reward such as a badge or certificate is likely to ensure continued appropriate behaviour and performance, as well as to increase the pupil's self-esteem and confidence.

It will surely be recognised that these ideas are grounded in the premise that we learn by being influenced or conditioned by the environment, be that another person or the physical environment. Some strategies devised for the teaching of PE which are based on this philosophy will be considered in Chapter 4.

PRINCIPLES OF LEARNING THROUGH UNDERSTANDING

An alternative view of how we learn is held by the cognitive psychologists. Here, the opinion is that we do not learn just by being conditioned, manipulated by the environment, as this is far too simplistic. We are, these educationalists would argue, always attempting to make sense of what is happening to us. We are not mindless automatons but thinking, creative beings, and if as teachers we accept this premise, then we will devise alternative strategies to enable our pupils to learn. We will give thought to the variety of previous experiences they had before coming to us; and to focusing attention and perception; to the individual interpretation pupils may put on the language and ideas we introduce to them. As has already been pointed out, some pupils will already have learned the appropriate behaviour to adopt in a swimming pool whereas others will have no experience here at all. Responses to the lesson will be affected by these issues. Some pupils have had a role model in the person of their adult carer, whilst others have never seen anyone in the water and so have no previous experiences upon which to draw. For the latter, therefore, there is a greater need to describe strokes by using analogies coming from their everyday experiences.

Attention and perception are profoundly influenced by a variety of internal and external factors. Intense, novel, changing stimuli are likely to attract attention. Interest, basic needs, fatigue and attention needs are all, too, likely to affect responses. We all have a multitude of stimuli bombarding us at all times. In order to remain sane, we focus on only a few. When a new skill is being learned, a large number of teaching points is important, so some selection must be made. The teacher needs to help the pupil to understand which are the important cues. In swimming, when learning a new skill, attention to the feel of the movement is very important, so the pupil might be required to think of the backstroke arms as being like a windmill, or the legs in the front crawl as sounding like a motorboat engine. In most sports, more than one activity needs to be undertaken at once. Swimming is no exception and arm action, leg action and breathing all need attention eventually. Initially, the teacher needs to break down the elements of the stroke until the first becomes automatic, then the second is added, and so on.

The way in which we make sense of the world depends on all the sensory experiences we have. It was mentioned how varied are the experiences which pupils bring into school, and it follows that the ways in which pupils interpret what they seen and hear may vary quite dramatically. The Gestalt psychologists argue that we try to impose order and structure on what we see and experience. We try to make sense of stimuli in terms of both the present context and our previous experience. It is not unusual for more than one person who has been in a particular social function to give very different accounts of the event afterwards. So it is in the classroom – you may know the story of the young child who drew Mary, Joseph and the Babe being flown in an aeroplane by 'Pilot'. When teaching swimming, it is essential to present the material to be learned in terms of previous experience. (See again the list of analogies on pages 150–53 at the end of this text.)

The Gestalt principles also suggest that we learn best when presented with the *whole* picture. We then understand clearly what it is we are aiming for. This means that pupils should be shown visually the whole stroke towards which they are moving so that they can then make sense of the various parts which make it up. This might best be done through the use of video and/or charts, pictures. Advance organisers, or clear statements of what is to take place in the lesson, are also recommended to enable pupils to see their learning both as a whole and in context. These views are in direct contrast to those expressed in Chapter 3. The exact nature of the swimming material may influence the method chosen by the teacher. The learning style, too, of the pupil needs to be taken into account: some pupils will be holistic in their approach to learning, whilst others will be atomistic. The holistic-style learner needs to see and understand the whole and then break it down into its constituent parts, whilst the atomist works in the opposite direction, being concerned at the beginning with the tiny elements which will ultimately build up. This latter pupil is likely to be happier working in a Skinnerian approach, whilst the holistic learner will be happier in a discovery style. This means giving the pupils the opportunity to be active in their own learning, to discover skills and techniques for themselves. In swimming, they can be given the task, for example, of finding the best way to propel themselves across the pool, or the best way to keep their head above water. All swimming strokes can be taught in both styles.

Other psychologists of the Gestalt school also argue that understanding of how to perform a skill may well come through a flash of insight. Not only may the solution come suddenly after a period of calm reflection, but the learner will look for patterns, structures, regularities in the material. Give the pupils reasons, then, for performing the correct and most efficient technique.

MOTIVATION AND NEEDS

Many writers would argue that teaching should start with the 'needs' of the student. Although we should not ignore aims and what is deemed to be worthwhile, it is impossible to effectively motivate pupils without considering and understanding the students' needs. Effective teaching/learning is dependent on motivation, which in turn is dependent on the satisfaction of basic human needs.

The literature on human needs falls into two broad approaches: *physiological/psychological* and *social*. Maslow (1970) is possibly the most influential exponent who, in his hierarchy of needs, embraces both of these approaches. Maslow identified three classes of needs which all humans embody: *primary* (food, sleep and safety); *emotional* (love, security and self-esteem); and *social* (self-fulfilment). He argues that a basis of primary physiological needs for food, sleep and safety must be satisfied before any further learning can take place. It is self-evident that it is impossible for a student to progress confidently and safely in the water if these basic needs have not been satisfied in life prior to coming to swimming, as well as in the pool at the time of the experience.

This then forms a foundation on which a hierarchy of subsequent needs is built: safety; affiliation; self-esteem; self-actualisation. Each of these levels in turn must be satisfied before the pupil can progress further. The pupil needs to feel physically and psychologically safe in the pool. Routines for behaviour and entry establish a feeling of safety. Then, the pupil needs to feel safe within the water itself. As already indicated, pupils come to school with different experiences and so require very different ways of satisfying their needs. It may be that equipment such as lane or width ropes need to be used in order that the pupil can feel safe in a 4′ 6″ (1.37 metres) pool. There is a fundamental and early need for a pupil to feel able to stand up after adopting either a prone or a supine position. For this reason, a pupil will often not take their feet off the bottom because they do not know how to stand up again and/or roll over. Confidence must be gained to enable the face to be immersed and breathing to be learned, to be able to lie back in the water and cope with the face getting wet, and for the body alignment to be efficient. As already mentioned, those pupils fortunate enough to have been taken as a baby will already have learned this confidence. Care needs to be taken to ensure that the pupil is not frightened early in the experience. Very early in the tuition process, the management of breathing must be taught. When being attacked or being put in a life-threatening situation such as approaching a burglar in the house at night, the instinctive reaction is to hold one's breath. So it is in swimming: the tense, nervous swimmer will hold their breath. The teacher must use imagination and creativity to conceal frightening tasks in water. Give the pupil fun activities such as blowing bubbles underwater, blowing table-tennis balls along and picking up objects from the bottom to develop confidence in the pupil without their realising. Early in the introduction of strokes, the emphasis must be placed on Blow as you go.

The emotional needs for affiliation can be satisfied through the use of group work, or working in pairs with one pupil guiding and helping the other; and participating in team games. Maslow's higher-order needs of self-esteem and self-actualisation can also be achieved through swimming. The degree of confidence that can be gained through mastery of the water is tremendous. There is then likely to be a carry-over of this confidence into other aspects of life, both academic and behavioural skills tending to improve as a consequence. Visual and imaginative skills can also be developed and used in other aspects of life.

Not only Maslow but other writers on the topic of motivation have also indicated that there would seem to be two main sources of motivation: *extrinsic* and *intrinsic*. Praise from the teacher, and tangible rewards such as badges etc., are illustrations of extrinsic rewards; and as was indicated earlier, one would hope that the *intrinsic* reward of pleasure in swimming for its own sake will then gradually take over, so that the child is then *internally* motivated to further their own development.

In swimming, it may be difficult at times to distinguish whether it is the 'pull' from without (extrinsic) or the 'push' from within (intrinsic) which is motivating. The body needs to be active for the primary-school-aged child has boundless energy. These internal physical forces need to be harnessed by the teacher of swimming to act as motivating forces to build up skill and technique. Exploration and curiosity, known by some as *attention needs*, are thought to be innate, and play is also thought by some to be an attention need. It would seem to be a universally spontaneous activity. Once a baby can move, they will actively explore their environment. Whatever the theories that have been propounded, primary teachers will be aware of the immense contribution play makes to meeting the physical, cognitive and social developmental needs of their pupils, and the teacher of swimming has only to harness these needs. There is every opportunity for these needs to be satisfied through this medium. Each and every lesson must be fully active, with an opportunity for the pupils to try out and discover their own best way of moving through water. Each lesson should have a contrasting activity which is fun and allows for play with an aquatic purpose. Watermanship activities also can give free rein to imaginative exercises (see Chapter 6).

Children need to succeed, but they may also have a fear of failure, and the balance of these two may be different in each individual. Whatever the source of this balance, teachers will have pupils in their classes who, to varying degrees, will have a fear of failure which in turn will determine the teacher's approach to a task set. Teachers need to know their pupils very well in order to be able to scale the physical demands in swimming to ensure that each pupil is able to succeed.

Research has begun to show that *goal-setting* can act as an important motivational force. According to Ewing *et al.* (1985), children between the ages of 9 and 11 seem to focus on mastery goals and social approval whereas a competitive goal is not fully developed until 11/12 years onwards. Buchan and Roberts (1991) have also found that boys are more competitive than girls. And the work that has been done by Ames (1988) would seem to suggest that pupils who see the goals in their classrooms as being primarily concerned with mastery and less on competition are more likely to be highly motivated and also more socially aware and co-operative. This would suggest that teachers of swimming need to set short-term goals to learn and develop personal skills. The pupils should also be made aware of their own achievements and be rewarded for them.

Thorpe (in Lee 1995) suggests that appropriate challenges which motivate some pupils may have the reverse effect on others. He therefore suggests setting goals which are 'within the control of the individual, i.e. personal performance goals'. The research undertaken by Jean Whitehead into the variety of common goals which children have for their sporting achievements, including social approval, links with the above in suggesting that teachers need to know what success means to the pupils in their classes. Only then may they be fully motivated not only to achieve in school but also to have the confidence to participate in sport throughout adult life.

Group work

According to the Programme of Study for Key Stage 2, 'Pupils should be taught to develop confidence in water and how to rest, float and adopt support positions; the principles and skills of water safety and survival' (Department for Education, 1995). It is a general requirement, too, of the Physical Education National Curriculum that pupils be taught 'to observe . . . good sporting behaviour as . . . team members . . .' (Department for Education, 1995). Many of these principles and skills are most appropriately taught through fun and games like activities. Games may be an extension of watermanship activities requiring more control and co-operative behaviour. Simple games using aids and apparatus such as soft balls may be profitably introduced early in the teaching programme.

As skill develops, these games require pupils to work not only in pairs but also in groups. Groups are likely to exist in some form in every classroom. Much of the academic work in primary classes takes place at least with the pupils sitting in group formation. Whether true group interaction is taking place here is a disputed argument, but working in groups does give the opportunity for pupils to develop skills of communication and co-operation as well as to practice leadership skills. Well-organised and structured group work has immense value for social education. However, care must be taken to ensure that pupils are made to interact positively for those benefits to ensue. It is not sufficient for pupils merely to be positioned adjacent to one another. Research would suggest that leadership is a feature of the activity and skill level rather than of personality. This would suggest that all pupils should be given the opportunity to take and exercise leadership. In the pool, pupils can be required to devise their own competitive three-vs.-three game involving a soft ball and four hoops, for example (C. Hardy, 1994). In groups, they can make up relay games using different numbers of pool widths and different strokes. Since these activities (suggested in Hardy, 1994) require choosing a team leader, the opportunity should be provided for this position to rotate.

The simple games and activities as well as the simple races suggested by Helen Elkington and Joan Harrison in *Teaching Physical Education* and in Chapter 6 of this text all require team communication, co-operation and leadership. The literature tells the teacher to ensure that the pupils are physically positioned to be able to communicate, in a circle for instance. Should a leader need to dominate the situation, then this individual needs to be either in the centre of the circle or the focus point of a segment of a circle.

The skills of essential communication should also be readily available to the pupil, whether verbal or physical. Distinctions between various uses of communication need to be taught. Pupils should be encouraged to signal through means other than shouting when in a team situation; arm signalling, for instance, should indicate the desire for possession of an implement. Undue shouting taking place in any Physical Education lesson can easily lead to a breakdown in discipline and control.

STYLES AND STRATEGIES TO COPE WITH INDIVIDUAL DIFFERENCES

A *teaching strategy* generally means a specific tactic chosen to achieve a specific aim, whilst a *teaching style* generally refers to the accumulation of strategies commonly used by a teacher. Earlier on in this book, it was claimed that every teacher has their own philosophy of teaching, even though this may not be articulated. It is hoped that by reading through the previous chapters and seeing the alternative philosophies put forward by different educationalists writing in the field, the teacher will be able to revise and refine their own personal philosophy. The reason for this hope is that strategies which the teacher will choose to use to deliver the PE curriculum will depend on that very philosophy.

There is a wide range of strategies available to the teacher to enable them to impart the desired information to pupils. Despite Sue Capel's (1996) claim that there could be a restriction on the range of teaching styles used in PE, I hope teachers will come to realise that although there is an emphasis on sport in the Physical Education National Curriculum (PENC), there is in fact a range of styles available to the teacher in swimming. As Sue Capel also recognises, pupils learn as much from the *way* in which PE is taught as from the *content* of the subject. We have already suggested to teachers that they need to take into account the different experiences pupils have received, and this means that they will need to devise different strategies to impart the required knowledge and skills in swimming.

The Mosston spectrum of teaching styles

In 1986, the British Association Of Advisers and Lecturers in Physical Education (BAALPE) National Study Group inaugurated a research project investigating different approaches used in the teaching and learning of Physical Education. As the basis of their investigation, they used the work of Mosston (1981). Mosston has devised a spectrum of teaching styles ranging from the *command style* through to the *self-teaching style* (see Table 4.1). As the spectrum progresses, the learner gradually becomes more independent, and the teacher less important. In addition, the focus of the style of the teacher modifies from being concerned with motor development initially through social development, personal development and cognitive development, to a final integration of all these developmental aspects. Clearly, the focus, objectives aims, and thus the philosophy of the teacher, will vary according to the style chosen. Ideally, the teacher will choose the style which most nearly exemplifies both their own philosophy and the needs of their pupils.

The study undertaken through BAALPE covered the full range of PE activities: gymnastics, dance, games, athletics, swimming, and outdoor and adventurous activities. The lessons in swimming were taught in the *inclusion style* where pupils are helped to appreciate their own strengths and weaknesses, assess their own performance and maximise their own improvement. Differentiated tasks are set by the teacher, and the pupil then chooses at what level to start work. The final evaluation of this style records that these pupils gained great enjoyment from working in this way. Although there appeared to be no significant improvement in technical ability, the inclusion groups were more involved in decision-making and were more aware of their strengths and weaknesses. Many of the weaker swimmers had to be helped to make judgements on their own abilities initially. If one's philosophy were concerned with social and cognitive development, then one would choose this as a style to adopt.

Although this is the only style used for swimming in that project, and whilst many teachers of swimming seem to be more at home with the command style, it is easy to see how the other styles could be adopted by the teacher of swimming. Reference has already been made in this text to aspects of the *reciprocal style*. Here, the pupils work in pairs, evaluating each other's performance. The teacher works with the pupil teacher in order to improve their evaluation and feedback. Clear criteria must be provided by the teacher – for example, 'Watch to see that the heels break the surface of the water.' Much social development is then encouraged in the pupil teacher in terms of observation, analysis, communication, awareness of others, patience and tolerance, so fulfilling the PENC requirement to 'make simple judgements about their own and other's performance'.

Style	Essential characteristics	Likely objectives
A: Command	• All decisions made by teacher • Learners do as told • Class responds as a group	• Conform to a single standard of performance • Efficient use of time to acquire skills • Safety and discipline
B: Practice	• Most decisions made by teacher • Learner makes some decisions at impact stage • Practice time on task set by teacher	• To improve skill • To make learners aware of relationship between practice time and skill level • To help learners judge level of performance
C: Reciprocal	• Planned by teacher, executed by learners • Learners work in pairs • One learner, one teacher, roles exchanged • Clear criteria, generally on cards, integral to style • Teacher works through pupil teacher	• To engage pupils in social situations to develop communication skills • To develop skills of observing, listening, analysing • To heighten patience, tolerance and awareness of others • To provide maximum feedback for performer
D: Self check	• Planned by teacher • Performance criteria essential • Pupils check own performance	• To help learners assess own performance • To help honesty and ability to be objective • To help pupils recognise own limitations
E: Inclusion	• Planned by teacher • Pupils check own performance, starting at own level and then progressing • Tasks set to highlight pupil progress	• To maximise involvement • To accommodate individual differences • To help pupils rationalise aspirations • To enable everyone to succeed

Style	Essential characteristics	Likely objectives
F: Guided discovery	• Teacher plans target which they lead pupils to discover • Questioning by teacher is fundamental • Appropriate steps in discovery process are critical • Redirect pupils who go off target	• To engage learners in convergent process of discovery • To develop sequential discovery skills • To develop patience
G: Problem solving	• Teacher presents questions or problem situation • Alternative solutions required • Organised into groups to share thinking • Pupils contribute to decisions at all stages	• To develop ability to work on problems and solve them • To develop insights into structures of activities • To develop ability to verify solutions • To encourage independent thinking • To promote learners' confidence
H: Individual programme	• Learner plans and designs programme • Teacher proposes subject matter and approves programme	• To encourage independent planning • To reveal levels of understanding • To encourage persistence • To promote self-confidence
I: Learner initiatives	• Learner selects content, plans and designs programme • Teacher approves programme • Learner executes programme and submits evaluation to teacher	• To encourage and develop independence • To display understanding • To encourage acceptance of personal responsibility • To develop self-confidence
J: Self-teaching	Pupil is both teacher and learner, working fully independently	

Table 4.1 *The Mosston spectrum of teaching styles*
Source: BAALPE, 1989

The *practice style* exemplifies the philosophy of the behaviourists. It is similar to the command style, but more responsibility is given to the pupils to practise on their own, whilst the teacher is then 'freed' to coach individuals – e.g. 'Keep practising on your backs, thinking about your arms brushing your ears and toes breaking the surface of the water. Stop when you need to recover and then keep going.'

The *self-check style* requires pupils to know the criteria for a good performance and to be able to evaluate their own performance against these. If the teacher follows the above advice in stroke analysis, then this style should follow. It should help them to 'cope with success and limitation in performance' and 'practise, improve and refine performance, and repeat series of movements they have performed previously, with increasing control and accuracy. They sustain energetic activity over appropriate periods of time, and demonstrate that they understand what is happening to their bodies during exercise' (National Curriculum Programme of Study, in Department for Education, 1995).

Mosston's later styles require pupils to be even more independent and to discover solutions to problems themselves. These styles rely on a philosophy of activity, with the individual being curious, creative and exploratory. Problems will be set by the teacher for the pupils to resolve, leading on to the pupils being able to devise and set their own programmes of learning.

Mawer's guidance cycle

Another psychologist who has investigated the ways in which teachers approach their tasks, has devised for the more effective practitioner a *guidance cycle*. In this, Mawer (1995) recommends that the teacher observe the pupil's performance and then give praise with constructive feedback. Mawer was very concerned about the fact that his observations had shown that the majority of teachers did not know whether or not their feedback had had any effect, so for Mawer, the teacher must then wait to observe the repetition of the action in order to make further comment, and hopefully give praise for the correct execution of the skill. This guidance cycle will then ensure improvement and subsequent learning. The cycle tends, however, to be alien to the teacher's natural teaching style, as Mawer noticed: the teacher tends to move on to the next pupil before ensuring that the improvement has taken place. For the most effective teaching to take place, it is vital that the teacher observe to see that the correct improvement has taken place. As the skill of operating the guidance cycle increases, so the pupils will still have the same amount of the teacher's attention. If classes in swimming are organised so that pupils work in pairs, with each of the two people observing and commenting on each other, then the teacher can operate the guidance cycle and one pupil can reward the other. The pupil teacher can be given a key teaching point upon which to work, for example, 'Can you see the heels break the surface of the water?' in the front crawl. In this example, as in other instances, the teaching point needs to be phrased within the limitations of the pupils' ability to observe and understand. This also has the merit of fulfilling the End of Key Stage Descriptors for Key Stages 1 and 2: 'They improve their performance through practising their skills, working alone and with a partner. They talk about what they and others have done, and are able to make simple judgements' (Stage 1). 'They make simple judgements about their own and others' performance, and use this information to improve the accuracy, quality and variety of their own performance' (Stage 2) (Department for Education, 1995).

Pupil attention and perception

In Chapter 3, the notion of attention and perception being fundamental underlying principles of learning was introduced. This idea would require the teacher to make sure that all pupils have their attention focused on them as the instructor and on the information that those pupils need to acquire. Sunlight, interesting activity in another part of the pool, sounds from elsewhere, can all attract attention away from the essential learning. Make sure, therefore, that all pupils are looking in the correct direction, and that they are silent and listening. At times, make use of an appropriate loud noise such as a tambour to encourage correct rhythm, vary pace and emphasis of delivery of instructions, and change activities to stimulate interest. Be sensitive also to fatigue setting in, particularly with younger pupils. Consider the length of lesson carefully, but also make sure that too long is not spent on one aspect of swimming which requires the use of the same muscles. Look carefully at the chapters on stroke analysis to see how the progressions of strokes can be built up without overtiring the leg muscles for example. Make a visual demonstration of the aspect of the stroke the pupils are learning. Position this demonstration so that all can see. Ask the class what it is they are to look at before the demonstration takes place and then talk through the demonstration as it takes place, making absolutely sure that all are paying attention.

Group composition and teacher numbers

It may well be that the teacher is faced with a class of pupils of very mixed abilities in swimming, ranging from the extremely competent through to the non-swimmer. This is a very difficult situation for one teacher to address. The pupils will need to be grouped according to ability, and ideally there will be one teacher for each group. Each group will need a unit of work and separate lesson plans to cater for their different needs. Mixed-ability teaching in swimming is rarely totally satisfactory. There may well be economic and practical restrictions which mean additional teachers are not possible, but one teacher per group should nonetheless be the ideal aim.

THE PRACTICE OF
SWIMMING

Setting the scene

Before the children swim, they need to receive instruction on safety, hygiene and care of equipment.

POOL SAFETY AND HYGIENE

These are covered in detail in the later section on water safety – please see pages 121–28.

EQUIPMENT

There are many swimming aids. These are invaluable, and the children should be given ample opportunity to experiment and practise. The aids create interest, the support gives confidence, and the excitement of movement adds to the fun of the lesson.

Apparatus should be selected to meet the needs of your children. They must be safe, with stimulating bright colours and a shape, texture and function that interferes as little as possible with movement. Adaptability is also an asset, and can be valuable in work with disabled children.

When purchasing equipment, consideration should be given to:

- support
  - beginners to enable them to experience early success;
  - in learning new skills;
  - during corrective practices.

- to aiding technical understanding:
  - in isolation practices, i.e. part practice (e.g. kicking tasks to appreciate the maximum propulsion gained by arms and legs);

- breathing practices can be undertaken, and a swimming aid enables the child to concentrate on the breathing phase of individual strokes.

● aiding propulsion:

- flippers, for example, provide an immediate increase in travel speed in the crawl strokes and dolphin butterfly. The flexible flipper highlights the value of flexible ankles.

● fun objects:

- ideal for contrasting activity in lessons. Swimming aids can be used with imagination. The attraction of toys for young children is great and can help to overcome many fears. The possibilities are endless. They can be blown along, picked up or used to swim round, under, onto, through etc.

Some suggested aids are as follows:

● *tummy bands*. There are different sizes and many variations here. The band must be secure so that it does not slip. As the child becomes more confident, the number of buoyancy floats on the tummy band can gradually be reduced.

● *rubber rings*. These are not as popular now as tummy bands, but if used there are different sizes: small, medium and large. The rubber ring should be secured so that it does not slip down to the knees. A tape running over the shoulder and tied to the ring is suitable. The tummy band and rubber ring enable the learner to move around, working on whole or part of a stroke. A tummy band is particularly useful when learning or correcting the breaststroke leg action.

● *arm bands*. There are different sizes here also. Some have double chambers, others single and even just a flat, disk-type band. The disks do not have to be inflated. Inflatable bands should have secure stoppers.

The armband can impede movement, so where possible, the armband with a flat section designed to be worn on the inner side of the arm for free movement, should be used.

The armband gives buoyancy, and this can be reduced as the beginner improves. The non-swimmer/beginner can work happily on various movements in the water. The teacher can work with a class of children wearing armbands, whereas a class of beginners without armbands progress more slowly, which is disappointing for pupil and teacher.

● *floats*. These should be made of foam material, which is safer than polystyrene. Children should be discouraged from picking or biting chunks out of this aid. A float about 25 cm long and 5 cm thick is better for children. The larger float is used for the more advanced swimmer.

● *buoyancy suit*. A very individual aid, this can encourage a more horizontal position, and is particularly useful for disabled children.

- *hoops and toys.* Hoops can be floating on the surface, or vertically just under the surface, or on the pool bottom. There are various sizes, and they can be used to swim around or – when underwater – through.

  Toys, balls, ducks, boats etc. are ideal for pushing or blowing along.

- *sinking objects and bricks.* Objects can be recovered from the pool bottom. With bricks, an ideal weight for younger children is 2 kg. The children can be set tasks underwater, and this encourages them to open their eyes and orientate themselves.

- *buoyancy and neck support.* Useful for disabled swimmers. The ring will help to support the head in water.

- *pole and noose.* A broom handle with a courlene rope threaded through a hosepipe to form a loop will support the body in prone or supine position.

- *egg flip.* This is a small plastic toy shaped like a flying saucer. The children blow it along, and if they blow hard, it 'flips' over. They are used to encourage blowing out through the mouth and nose at the surface of the water, and for gaining confidence at putting the face in the water.

- *pull buoys, hand paddles/fins.* These are used by more advanced swimmers for pulling sweeps with strike skills to *strengthen* the arms.

- *markers.* Reels of courlene rope and also yachting buoys are invaluable for marking off pool areas either widthways or lengthways.

- *music.* This creates an relaxing atmosphere and aids co-ordination. It is also used for games, providing *variety* and enjoyment. Poolside equipment must be battery-powered.

- *whiteboard.* This provides visual explanation, showing movement in words. Used for able swimmers, it enables the teacher to set a group a task and then move freely and help others.

- *clock.* With a sweep second hand, this is useful for chain swimming, recover-type-survival and speed work, timing swims etc.

- *percussion.* A small drum to beat out rhythms is also very useful.

- *charts/videos/computers.* Clear accurate pictorial guidance can enhance poolwork. Poolside videos provide instant visual feedback and a record of progress. Ideal for skills analysis and for storing lesson plans, registers and progress reports.

It is important for the children to be taught to look after equipment, and to *tidy up* and *store* equipment after the lesson. This should become a ritual, and they will soon appreciate looking after belongings etc.

THE ENVIRONMENT

The following points should be borne in mind:

1   The water and the surrounding air temperature should be comfortable – the water temperature ideally around 27 °C (80 °F), with the air temperature slightly higher to prevent excessive humidity.

2   There should be ample room in the pool for the class size. Many Local Education Authorities stipulate a maximum class size in the range of 20 to 25 children per teacher.

3   A lesson a day for three weeks is better than a lesson a week for 15 weeks. Lessons at first should be short, e.g. 15 to 20 minutes, with plenty of movement.

4   The dimensions of the pool must obviously be suited to the children's age and ability. Nursery and infant children can be taught in shallow pools, and many schools now have teaching pools. A shallow pool is admirable initially, but once the children are swimming, more depth is needed and it is worth having a pool which can be filled to about one metre. A pool on one depth (no deep or shallow end) is preferable.

5   The pool and all apparatus should be made as attractive as possible, with bright colours. Imaginative designs on the pool walls and bottom can contribute greatly. The colour, shape, size and texture of apparatus all intrigue the young and add to the fun of their activities.

6   The pool should have a removable teaching rail.

7   Changing rooms must be warm.

8   Small children often have problems in putting their clothes on pegs and keeping them together. An excellent idea is to have the children put their clothing into shoe bags.

9   Showers, foot baths and toilets must be clean. Attitudes to hygiene and safety should be reinforced in swimming lessons. Pupils should help to maintain both their own personal hygiene and the cleanliness of the facilities.

10 An alarm system should be available in all pools. There must be a suitable warning device for pupils in the water (e.g. a siren or hooter), safety poles available, and quick access to a telephone.

Early lessons and fundamentals

Parents can do much to familiarise children with water. Babies can be introduced to it by playing in the bath at home. A child of a few months will benefit tremendously from having made friends with water, for by the time they reach the nursery school or their first swimming lesson, they know what to expect. It helps if the child's mother or father (in the early stages) introduces them to the swimming pool. A petrified child has invariably been frightened or put off earlier in life. Parents must guard against this.

It is very important for nursery, infant and primary-school-age children to be taken swimming. Although there are problems with timetabling, expense, staffing, transport and helpers to dress and undress the very small, parents can often help. No child should enter senior school as a non-swimmer.

By the time the child is six or so, they are able to understand and co-ordinate movements and are at an ideal age to learn the basic essentials of strokes. Remember, children differ in learning ability just as they vary physically, intellectually and emotionally. A natural ability must be allowed to develop.

One must not be dogmatic about teaching methods. The facilities available, the frequency and length of lessons and the pupils' abilities must all be taken into account. Pupils must also have ample opportunity to experiment and discover. The teacher can give guidance in three main ways: verbally, visually and manually. In all instances, the pupil must be successful if interest is to be maintained. If the pupils are in a pool which is not large, the whole point of the lesson can be lost if the teacher does not organise the space properly. It is often best to divide the class into sets of two. 'Number ones' swim across the pool, and when they reach halfway, 'twos' follow in the same path. The 'ones' then arrive at the opposite side and pause until the 'twos' arrive, and then the number 'ones' return and the procedure is repeated. This prevents overcrowding and large gaps in the lesson.

THE FIRST STAGE

The beginners' class

A class of beginners is one of the most exciting, enjoyable and challenging experiences – an ideal class, bubbling with enthusiasm and desperate to learn. All that the children require is guidance in the skills, and progress is soon evident. A few will be apprehensive, but these pupils are in the minority. A lot of apparatus should be used, and in a large pool a courlene rope should mark off a safe area to ensure that children do not stray out of their depth. Some children do not like the splash of others in the group and are loath to try strokes with so much water disturbance. A second rope is an advantage, enclosing a small area at the very shallowest part of the pool; as confidence grows, this can be removed.

Children may work away from the rail in the early lessons and try out activities for themselves: the value of partner support work is questionable at this stage, particularly one beginner supporting another, because (*a*) it wastes the time of one child, (*b*) the supporting partner gets cold and (*c*) the support is invariably incorrect and confidence can therefore be lost.

The following approach is successful, and are progressions which can be attempted in the first lesson and repeated in the following two or three.

1 *Before the lesson,* make sure each child has a suitable-size tummy band and armbands .

2 *Entry* can involve the pool steps or be from a sitting position on the bathside. For the second method, i.e. the swivel entry, the pupil sits on the poolside with both legs/feet hanging free of the trough or rail. If they wish to turn, for example, to their left, the *left* hand is placed on the poolside and grips the edge. The right hand reaches across the body and is also placed on the poolside. Both hands press down, the pupil swivels the body and it is lowered into the water.

3 *Spread* the children out in the water and get them to stretch their arms sideways, looking upwards and bending the knees. This is important: it shows the children how to space themselves out and bend their knees because, once in the water, their shoulders must be underneath to help general stability, with the arms stretched sideways for balance and the eyes looking upwards to prevent toppling forwards.

4 *Movement.* The children with bent knees, shoulders underwater (this is

essential), arms stretched sideways, eyes looking upwards. They weave in and out of one another using all the space available. They should experiment, with their feet moving forwards, backwards and sideways. This enables them to discover how to transfer their weight in order to move efficiently – moving forwards from heel to toe, or back from toe to heel, or side-stepping. The size of the steps can vary – the teacher can ask 'What size steps help you to move quickly?' As the children move, the teacher should encourage them to put their faces in the water: 'You have a black spot on your nose. Draw large patterns in the water – circles, squares, triangles.' A drum can be most effective at this stage: the children move in time to the beat and change direction on a heavier beat. I find this is most successful at getting children involved and overcoming any reservations they might have. Music with a good rhythm is also useful. Coloured balls are good for interest too: the children blow or push them along with their noses, head or hands. Their feet will begin to lift slightly from the pool bottom.

5   *Buoyancy.* The children must be able to float on their fronts (prone) and on their backs (supine), roll over and stand up. They spread their arms wide, look upwards and imagine they are going to sit down. As they do this, they discover both feet lifting off the bottom. Repeat this several times. The children should now be shown how to plant their feet firmly back on the bottom if they are launched onto their fronts or backs. The pupils should be taught to roll from their backs to their fronts, and vice versa. Children respond very well through their imagination – 'They think of a piece of toast. You are going to make yourselves as brown a you can.' They usually stretch their arms and legs and turn over like a pancake, and they are floating! 'Try to get both sides toasted.' Then: 'One small part of you only is going to get toasted – make yourselves smaller.' This latter instruction brings about a tuck shape or a thin narrow shape. The teacher can thus bring about a useful transfer between the three common shapes: wide/wall, narrow/pin, tuck/ball. Finally: 'Who can get toasted on one side and roll over and get toasted on the other side?'

6   *Propulsion.* There is no reason why pupils with tummy bands and armbands should not experiment with arm actions and discover how to pull themselves through the water. They will use either a *dog paddle* – a long pull with alternate arms starting in an extended position in front of their faces and pulling right through to touch the hips or, still on the front, a simultaneous movement with hands and arms held firmly to push the water aside, like swimming through long grass or thick mud. Let them blow out as they move about, and say to them that the motto for the day is 'Blow as you go!' (The *blowing out* is initially more important than the *inbreath.* A good blow out will be automatically followed by breathing in.)

This prevents the 'blue' faces and bursting cheeks common to all non-swimmers trying desperately to concentrate on their new skills.

A kick can be added to the dog-paddle arm action, but the breaststroke kick should be taught carefully before co-ordinating it with simultaneous arm action. Some children love kicking alternately on their backs, which is fine as they are learning the first stage of an alternative stroke in which breathing occurs very much more easily.

7   *Submerging.* The pupils vary in their reaction to underwater activity. Tummy bands must be removed – and armbands usually, too. Weighted hoops are placed in different areas of the shallow end. 'Find different ways of getting through your hoop – head first, feet first, sideways etc.' Bricks and flippers can be picked up from the pool bottom. If the child finds difficulty in sinking, experiment with the *speed* of submerging, i.e. 'Tuck up and sit quickly and blow out as you do so.' Or the teacher can hold a pole at the poolside for the pupil to climb down hand over hand – like a monkey or like a fireman. 'Which part of your body can you rest on the bottom of the pool?' (head, seat, knees, hands, feet, hip, tummy, back etc.). 'Run round to the drumbeat, and on every heavy beat sit on the bottom of the pool.'

The timid pupil

The timid pupil requires individual help, and it is usually necessary to help them at a time when the pool is quiet – generally outside lesson times. Once the pupil has experienced some success this fear will begin to go and more adventurous tasks can be attempted until they can eventually participate in a class lesson. The teacher can instill confidence in any timid non-swimmer both by support given manually and by appropriate verbal encouragement.

Possible activities with the pupil wearing a rubber ring and armbands are these:

1   *Entry.* The teacher enters the water first via the pool steps, demonstrating how to enter correctly (turning at the top of the steps with the back to the pool, and looking down to see that the feet are firmly placed), *or* enters the water and lifts the pupil into the pool.

2   The teacher holds the pupil firmly. The teacher's and pupil's shoulders should be underwater, and the pupil should slide their feet along the pool bottom to get the feel of movement. After this, the feet should be lifted and pressed firmly back on the bottom of the pool. The pupil should be asked simple questions – 'Which part of your foot do you put on the ground?' – and encouraged to *walk* forwards, backwards, sideways.

3   The teacher alters the support. The pupil extends the arms sideways, and looks upwards. Both feet should be lifted a few inches off the pool bottom

and then replaced. This should be repeated several times. The support of the teacher should eventually be removed, the pupil should then try the task unsupported. Can the knees be tucked to the chest?

4   The teacher supports the child on the *front*, and they begin to kick their legs. This is then repeated, and the child has go on the *back*.

5   The teacher should show the pupil how to launch onto the front or back, stand up or roll over in the water. No pupil will feel secure until they can do these things. The pupil will now be doing well, and will feel happier. The teacher, talking gently, should now encourage a kick on the front and back.

6   Use a coloured ball and encourage the pupil to push it along with the hands, nose or head. This is a real achievement since the pupil will now be working without support.

7   The lesson could conclude with the pupil lying in a floating star shape position on their back in the water. Can they change to a thinner or tucked shape?

The timid child's individual lesson should be short but full of variety. (We would suggest 10 to 15 minutes.)

With patience and understanding from the teacher, success will follow. The timid pupil should then progress to the activities suggested for the beginners' class.

THE SECOND STAGE

The children are now ready to progress to a more advanced stage. The following are some possibilities:

1   *The multi-stroke artificial aid lesson.* Teachers should not impose their favourite stroke on the children. There has been success in the earlier lessons, and interest must be maintained. It can be very disheartening if a child is forced to work on a stroke which they are unable to cope with; for example, not every child can cope with the breaststroke, which requires flexible ankles. Consider the ideas in Chapter 3.

    The multi-stroke artificial aid approach is educationally sound. Here, the pupils wear tummy bands and armbands and hold floats. The leg action of the four main strokes – i.e. the front and back crawl, breaststroke and dolphin butterfly stroke – can be introduced. The children experiment and discover for themselves the kick most suited to them. They can then proceed to work on their kick and breathing, and remove aids and progress to arm strokes as confidence grows.

2   *The shallow water method.* This method can be used with infants or primary-

school-age children. The pool needs to be 30–45 cm *constant* depth. The pupil can then move around on the front or back using hands on the pool bottom to propel, balance and support them. Artificial aids need not be used.

3   *The flipper float method.* This is a suitable method for individual tuition. The pupil lies in the prone or supine position with a rubber ring, armbands and flippers, and holding one or two floats. The stretched position can be achieved with the support of a large noose suspended on a broom handle held by the teacher. This noose should be placed under the armpits of the prone swimmer, and under the shoulder blades or the back of the neck for a swimmer on their back. The swimmer kicks, and as confidence grows, the noose can be lowered. With the aid of the flippers, the swimmer travels rapidly forwards, no longer requiring the extra support.

This is not an ideal method for an infant or primary-school class, but while most of the children are learning by one of the other methods, one or two individuals might benefit from the flipper float method to get them moving initially. If a pupil tends to overbend the knees when kicking, the flippers also often help to straighten the leg and encourage a swing from the hip.

4   *The whole–part–whole method.* Many new skills are learnt easily by the whole–part–whole approach where the pupils are first shown the *whole* stroke they are about to work on. Basic guidance is given by the teacher, and the pupils then try it for themselves. Their efforts will probably initially appear very rough, but the idea is for the pupils to feel the whole movement and rhythm of the stroke. They then progress to *part* practice with the stroke broken down into sections, e.g. leg action, arm action, or arm action and breathing co-ordinated. The pupil finally returns to the *whole* stroke, and hopefully, improvement is evident. (See Chapter 3.)

The whole–part–whole approach is favoured by many. Our preference is to build a stroke on a sound leg kick since in the initial stages the kick can greatly affect the body position, stability, propulsion and general rhythm.

GAME ACTIVITIES

'Play with a purpose' is an ideal method of getting used to water and developing confidence. Activities can take place underwater and on the surface, and if they are made challenging and exciting, the children will progress in many ways.

It is important to ensure the children are happy in water by working along the lines we have mentioned above *before* 'regimenting' them into several weeks of work on specific strokes. But they should eventually be taught the correct way to swim each stroke once they have experienced the thrill of water as a medium to move in. The following are some suggestions for games.

1 *Underwater* (aids should be removed for underwater games):

- Weighted hoops, bricks, coffee-jar tops and flippers can be picked up from the bottom of the pool.
- Certain objects can be used to swim through, round and onto, e.g. hoops, weighted skittles and mats.
- A very effective game is to get the children to swim or walk and, on a whistle or drumbeat, to submerge and pick up an object. I have tried this to music too, and it is even more exciting for the children. It works like musical chairs: when the music stops the children submerge. Or the children can sing 'Ring a Ring of Roses', submerging on 'we all fall down!'.
- 'Who can stand on their hands?' 'Who can kneel?' 'Who can sit?' This will encourage many children to submerge, and the teacher keeps them moving by telling them to move from one part of the pool to another before surfacing.
- Swimming underwater (for those able to swim) individually. 'How many ways can you find of swimming underwater?' 'What helps to keep you down as you swim?'
- 'Pretend you are making a cup of tea underwater.'
- Washing the face and hair and blowing bubbles into the water. Encourage the pupils to keep their eyes open.
- Climbing through or swimming through a hoop submerged just below the water surface.
- Touching the bottom with various parts – e.g. elbow, knee or hip.

2 *Above water* (aids can be used):

- Blowing, nosing or heading objects across the width of the pool.
- Blowing a ball across the width and around floating objects, e.g. buoys.
- A *scull* across the pool (sculling is described in the backcrawl stroke section on page 51 in Chapter 7) on the back, with a float resting on the tummy.
- Pushing a float to the opposite side of the pool or swimming around a buoy or an object to return to the starting side.
- 'Mr Shark'. The class all spread out behind a leader and start walking across the pool behind the leader. The children keep saying 'What's the time, Mr Shark?', and the leader gives a time. The children go on until the reply is 'Dinnertime!'. Then they have to turn tail and reach the poolside before they are touched.

- Ropes can be useful. The children can follow a leader, pulling themselves across the pool. This is a particularly useful activity for some disabled swimmers.

- Shopping – collecting a variety of floating objects onto a float and bringing them to the side to the 'checkout'!

- Traffic policeman – each pupil faces the teacher (who is the traffic policeman) and must travel in the direction indicated. Pupils face the teacher at all times. This is excellent for encouraging the use of different directions.

- Simple ball games such as pushing a ball across the pool and putting it into a box at the side. Cup and ball races are fun too. Simple relays, involving passing balls from one to another, are also a possibility.

- Follow my leader is popular too, and everyone can take turns at being the leader.

FUNDAMENTALS

Buoyancy

The amount of air in the lungs, the shape of the body, the body position and the type of water a body is immersed in, all affect a person's ability to float.

There is a simple float called a *mushroom float* which demonstrates accurately how well a person can float. The pupil should get into the mushroom float position (see Figure 6.1) having taken in large breath which is then held. The body should float with part of the back visible above the surface. If the mushroom float is repeated and air is then forcibly exhaled, the body should

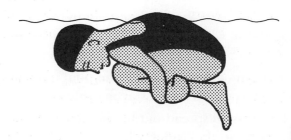

Figure 6.1 *The mushroom float*

sink. Pupils who experience this learn to appreciate how air in the lungs aids *buoyancy*.

Pupils come in all shapes and sizes – a body may be fat (endomorph), thin (ectomorph) or muscular (mesomorph) – body shape will affect the floating position – a person with a high proportion of fat – or *adipose tissue* – will usually float very easily in a horizontal supine position, whereas a muscular person may only be able to float in a vertical position with arms outstretched at the surface and well back. The way in which a body floats depends on the relationship between the *centre of buoyancy* (air and fatty tissue) and the *centre of gravity* (muscle and bone). For a body to float, it needs to have a *specific gravity* less than the water in which it is immersed. A human body has a specific gravity of 0.97–0.98, very close to the SG of fresh water, which is 1.00. Therefore, it is usually possible for a human body to float with only a small part of the body above the water surface. Salt water has a higher SG than fresh water and is therefore much easier to float in.

Pupils should be given the chance to experiment with floating in various positions. A lesson on buoyancy is of great value.

Propulsion and resistance

In order for a swimmer to swim faster, propulsion must be increased or resistance must be minimised – or both. In swimming, *propulsion* is obtained by the application of *force*. The required force is generated by the arms and legs of the swimmer. The force needs to be applied in the direction opposite to the one in which the swimmer wishes to go. This is an application of Newton's Third Law of Motion which states that for every action there is an equal and opposite reaction. This can be clearly demonstrated by a swimmer, supine, using a standard scull which presses the water towards the feet, enabling the swimmer to travel head first.

A greater degree of propulsion is obtained when a curved or elliptical pathway is followed. This is because the hand which uses an elliptical pathway is constantly moving into 'still' water, whereas the hand which follows a straight pathway moves with an ever-increasing mass of water, thus decreasing the propulsive force generated.

During the propulsive phase of the arms, it is vital for the hands to 'fix' in the water and not 'slip'. This 'fixing' takes place at catch point, i.e. just after the start of the underwater arm action when the swimmer feels water pressure, and every swimmer needs to feel that they have a 'hold' on the water at this point. The propulsive phase of all the arm strokes should be accelerating, especially during the latter part. Propulsion from the arms is more efficient if the arms are bent. This shortens the lever so that greater force can be applied. The hand acts as a paddle and needs to be held firmly. The pitch of the hand is constantly changing so that the hand is in the best position to apply force.

Resistance needs to be kept to a minimum, and one way of doing this is by keeping the body as *streamlined* as possible. Teachers can help their pupils to achieve maximum streamlining by working on controlling their body shape – i.e. or body awareness. Push and glide practices are an excellent way for swimmers to experience a streamlined horizontal swimming position. Frontal resistance will be excessive if a swimmer has poor streamlining. Obviously, a breaststroke swimmer will have greater frontal resistance than a front crawl swimmer due to the nature of the stroke, but it is important to keep frontal resistance to a minimum.

A well-fitting swimsuit also helps to lessen resistance, and the fabric from which it is made is also important. Wearing a swim cap also helps, especially if a swimmer has long hair. Some competitive swimmers shave off all their body hair in order to reduce frictional resistance (pupils need not do this, however!).

Profile resistance is affected by the size of the area which cuts into the water at the front end. This is perhaps best explained by thinking of a battering ram and a javelin. A javelin, which is tapered at the front, creates far less profile resistance than a battering ram, which presents a significant flat area at the front end, thus creating far greater profile resistance.

WATERMANSHIP

For some ideas here, see pages 39–47 above.

Sculling

Sculling has enormous value as a *watermanship* activity, as well as being a skill which can be used in association with the back-crawl leg kick and the inverted breaststroke kick. There are many sculls, but the ones that are most relevant to this book are:

- *head first* or *standard scull*
- *foot first* or *reverse scull*
- *flat* or *stationary scull*

Sculling propels the body through use of the hands and wrists. For the three sculls listed above, the swimmer lies in a supine position at the surface, with eyes looking up and tummy, hips and toes at the surface. The arms are held almost straight, close to and slightly beneath the hips. The hands move inwards and outwards at the wrist, with the hand being held firmly, fingers together and thumbs tucked in. Pressure is applied continuously in the opposite direction to that in which the swimmer wishes to travel. A firm, fast scull will give better propulsion and smoother travel along the water surface. For the stationary scull, there is also downward pressure to keep the swimmer afloat. In standard sculling, the pathway followed by the hand looks like a figure of eight turned on its side.

Plenty of practice is necessary to improve sculling, and a variety of approaches should be tried:

1 using a tambour or drum. Here, the pupil changes from one scull to another every time there is a heavy beat. The changes should be smooth and controlled.
2 using music – counting beats, and changing sculls every eight counts. Or using the phrasing in a piece of music to indicate when to change.

Once pupils have been taught the basic sculls, they can learn some gymnastic-type figures. In performing stunts, the arms which scull are used to propel, balance, turn, spin and control.

Tub

Begin with the body lying flat and still in the supine position. Use a flat scull at this point. The head is in line with the body, eyes looking up. The tummy and toes are up at the surface. The body is stretched. The arms are sculling by the sides. This position is called a *back layout*. Then the knees and lower legs are drawn along the surface of the water until the thighs are vertical. This is the tub position – make sure the head is back and the eyes are looking up. Using the seat as a pivot point, the pupil should smoothly rotate through 360 degrees in a clockwise direction. The sculling action is important. To rotate clockwise, the right hand should use a standard scull and the left hand should use a flat scull.

Somersault back tuck

Begin in a back layout position. The knees are drawn up towards the chest and the head is tucked in, making a very tight ball shape. The arms sweep forward, causing the body to rotate backwards. The body should stay near the surface of the water.

Oyster

Once again, begin in a back layout. Then, slide the arms out to the side and back, beyond the head. At this point, the arms need to be about 30 cm below the surface, with the palms of the hands facing up towards the surface. Then, simultaneously, press up with the extended legs and up with the straight arms in a firm thrusting-type movement. At the same time, pike at the hips, moving the body into a closed pike position. The body submerges in this closed pike position, staying in position until it is completely submerged.

Strokes

THE BACK CRAWL STROKE

The *back crawl* is an alternating stroke and is popular with many people as breathing here is easier due to the face being clear of the water.

Body position

The body should be on the back (*supine*) in a horizontal, streamlined position. It should be as flat as possible, with a slight slope down to the hips in order to keep the leg kick in the water. Only the toes break the surface.

It is important for the head to remain steady throughout the stroke. It should be held in line with the body, with the ears resting in the water. The eyes should look up. If the stroke is swum at speed, the head needs to be raised a little to stop a lot of water washing over the face.

In the early stages of learning the stroke, the shoulders need to be kept as steady as possible. However, in order for pupils to develop a more advanced technique, it is essential to develop a body roll around the longitudinal axis. The only part not involved in this body roll is the head, which needs to remain steady throughout. The body roll needs to be developed because:

  (i) it places the pulling arm lower into the water, enabling it to pull more efficiently;

 (ii) it causes the shoulder of the recovering arm to lift clear of the water, making the recovery easier;

(iii) a combination of (i) an (ii) improves the overall streamlining of the stroke.

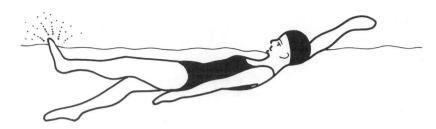

Figure 7.1 *Body position and leg action in the back crawl stroke*

Leg action

The *leg action* helps to maintain a good body position, balances the body and can propel the body especially if the swimmer has flexible ankles. The leg action is alternating and works mainly in the vertical plane, though when there is body roll, the legs will also work to some extent laterally in direct proportion to the amount of body roll at the hips. The legs should swing quite close together, and where there is good ankle flexibility, 'in-toeing' – i.e. turning the feet towards each other, particularly on the upward kick – will be seen.

Upkick

The *upkick* is initiated at the hips. At the start of the upkick, the knee is somewhat bent, and the pupil should feel the movement through hip, knee and foot. The movement upward accelerates especially through the lower leg, causing the leg to straighten. The upkick is completed with the leg fully extended and the toes at the surface.

Downkick

The *downkick* is a much more relaxed movement, initiated again at the hip. As the leg moves downward, the knee bends slightly and the foot reaches a depth of 30–45 cm.

Arm action

The continuous *arm action* provides most of the propulsion for the stroke. There are two types of arm pull action. The basic straighter arm pull (see Figure 7.2) and, for more advanced swimmers, the 'S' pull.

Basic back-crawl arm action

Arm action
The alternating arm action is ideal for propulsion and continuity. The continuous movement is often likened to a windmill (see Figure 7.4).

Entry
One arm enters the water in an extended position in advance of the head and in line with the shoulder. The little finger enters the water first. The wrist is held firmly and is flexed. (The swimmer imagines their hand is being placed on top of a shelf.)

Catch
A few inches underwater the wrist and hand should be firm. Avoid letting the hand collapse at this point.

Pull sweep
The arm is pulled in a semi-circular sweep in a shallow semi-circle. The thumb knuckle should be uppermost. Sweep to the hips. The pulling arm remains parallel to the water surface at a depth of 15–30 cm.

Recovery
The arm leaves the water with the thumb leading, slicing out of the water like a knife. The arm is extended and carried in a relaxed manner directly back to the entry position beyond the head. As the arm passes the rear, the arm rotates, turning the palm outwards so that it is in the correct position for entry.

The 'S' pull

Downsweep
After catch point, the hand sweeps downward and outward, and the shoulder of the pulling arm continues to roll into the water. This roll really allows the pupil to get a good propulsive action. After catch point, the movement begins to accelerate and continues to accelerate, reaching its maximum speed at the end of the second downsweep.

Upsweep
The hand now begins to sweep upward, inward and somewhat towards the feet. As it does so, the elbow flexes and by the end of the upsweep, the elbow bend is about 90 degrees. The upsweep finishes with the hand approximately level with the chest, palm slightly turned out and facing towards the feet. At this point, the hand is only just below the water surface.

Figure 7.2 *Basic arm action (from above) for the back crawl*

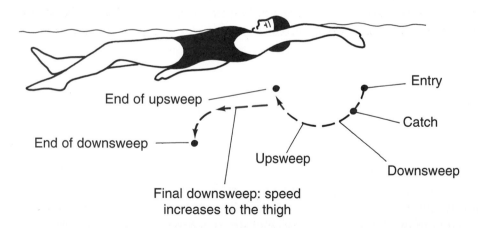

Figure 7.3 *The 'S' pull*

Downsweep

The hand now presses firmly towards the feet and inwards to the side of the body. It is a powerful action, and the elbow straightens throughout. At the end of this movement, the hand presses down hard, which lifts the shoulder ready for recovery. The hand finishes just under the hip, almost touching the thigh.

When the underwater propulsive phase of the stroke is viewed from the side, the pathway of the hand looks like the letter 'S' laid on its side.

Recovery
The arm leaves the water, with the thumb leading, slicing out of the water like a knife. The arm is extended and carried in a relaxed manner, directly back to the entry position beyond the head. As the arm passes the ear, the arm rotates inwards, turning the palm outwards so that it is in the correct position for entry.

This 'S' pull arm action (see Figure 7.3) is quite an advanced technique – allowing a more powerful and direct force over a longer period – and needs to be developed once the pupils can use a straight arm action correctly. In the straight arm pull, the arm, after entry, pulls in a shallow semi-circle with the thumb knuckle upper most, through to the hips. The pulling arm remains parallel to the water surface at a depth of 15–30 cm.

Breathing

Breathing in the back crawl presents no great difficulty as the face is clear of the water. It usually occurs once in every stroke cycle, and happens fairly automatically. When the arm on the breathing side starts its propulsive phase, breath is exhaled through the mouth and nose, and when the same arm commences its recovery, inhalation takes place. Breathing in the back crawl can be *trickle* or *explosive* (see pages 61–63 for definition of these terms).

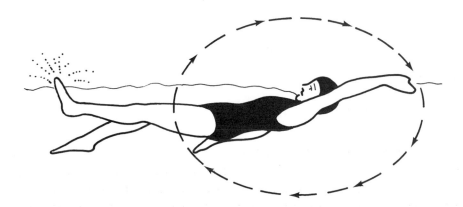

Figure 7.4 *The windmill action in the back crawl*

Timing

Once the technique of the back crawl has been mastered, it is a lovely, relaxed-looking stroke. It flows beautifully, and the movements of the arms are continuous like the action of a windmill (see Figure 7.4). Normally, there are six beats of the legs to each cycle of the arms. The overall impression of this stroke is one of smoothness and rhythm.

Table 7.1 *Causes and corrections for faults in the back crawl*

Fault	Hips low – piking of the body
Cause:	Lack of technique
Correction:	Push and glide – emphasise hips up and head back, ears in the water
Fault:	Head too high – held out of water
Cause:	Fear
	Lack of understanding of what is required
Correction:	Push and glide – head back, ears in the water
Fault:	Legs kicking too low
Cause:	Head raised too high
	Inadequate leg action
Correction:	Push and glide
	Early leg practices
Fault:	Excessive knee bend when kicking
Cause:	Lack of understanding
Correction:	Leg kick practices with float – encourage long, straight legs, swing from hip, tighten thigh muscle, stretch toes
Fault:	Wide entry of arms
Cause:	Lack of flexibility
	Lack of understanding
Correction:	Reteach arm action – encourage arm to brush ear at entry. Little finger enters first.
Fault:	Short propulsive phase
Cause:	Lack of understanding
Correction:	Arm practices – emphasise finish of propulsive phase at the hips
Fault:	Lack of continuity in arm action. A 'stop' in the stroke
Cause:	Weak leg action
	Lack of understanding of required 'windmill' action
Correction:	Leg practices to build up efficiency of kick
	Whole stroke work – emphasise continuous nature of stroke

Table 7.2 *Teaching the back crawl – suggested progressions*

Material	Teaching points	Organisation
1 Push and glide on the back and stand up	Hands hold side, shoulder-width apart Feet on wall, hip width apart Eyes look forward Forceful push-off Body stretched, arms by sides To stand up – arms press down and forwards Head forward – 'head a football' Hips back, knees bend and push down to the floor	Spread out along poolside in shallow area (Ensure it is safe to push off and that no-one will be in a collision)
2 a) Leg kick with two floats	Swing from the hips, legs stretched Legs swing close together: depth 30–45 cm; small splash, toes to the surface Steady rhythm Eyes look up, tummy up	Enough floats for the pupils to have two each One float held under each arm
b) Leg kick with one float	Teaching points as for previous practice	One float per pupil Float hugged to chest
c) Leg kick with standard scull	Teaching points as for previous practice Points for sculling: hands close to the sides; fingers together hands slightly cupped; fingers point upwards; move at wrist in a sideways figure of eight; push water towards feet; elbows straight	Work widthways
d) Leg kick, hands on thighs	Keep body stretched, tummy up	
(e) Leg kick, arms stretched beyond the head, hands clasped (This kick is a test of leg kick efficiency) (If the swimmer can manage this, the kick will be efficient)	Thumbs locked, ears squeezed between the arms Leg kick as above	

Material	Teaching points	Organisation
3 Arm action standing	Little finger enters the water first Hands firm, wrist slightly flexed Arms straight; keep thumb knuckle up during pull and push to hips Recovery direct and flowing Stand one foot in front of other, bend knees to keep shoulders in the water Lean back and get a steady rhythm	Standing in shallow water, one foot in front of the other Spread out, use the space
4 Whole stroke	Push and glide, then bring in the leg kick, then the arm action Teaching points as appropriate Natural breathing Continuous flowing action	Widthways
Once the pupil has mastered the back-crawl stroke as set out above, further practices can be used to develop the more advanced S-pull. These are set out below.		
Kick, roll to right then to left	Arms by the side Press right shoulder down, then left shoulder Keep a rhythmic kick going	
Single arm practices	Little finger entry, press hands down S-shaped sweep through to the hips Downsweep at the hip to lift the shoulder for recovery Accelerating action Roll into stroke Arm not being used is held by the side	
Single arm practices (one arm 1st length, other arm next)	Teaching points as appropriate Accelerating movement	Pupils use lane ropes *lengthways* to pull themselves along Follow the leader

THE FRONT CRAWL STROKE

The *front crawl* (see Figure 7.5) is a very popular stroke. It is a natural stroke, but its disadvantage is the fact that the face is in the water, which makes breathing difficult to master.

Body position

The body should be kept as near to the surface as possible for maximum streamlining, but there should be a slight slope to the hips in order to keep the leg kick in the water. Only the heels should break the surface. The face is in the water, with the head in line with the body; the eyes look forward and somewhat downwards. The *waterline* should be at the top of the forehead. The head is held steady, and rotation sideways in order to breathe should be smooth and rhythmic. A roll of the body around the longitudinal axis is desirable in more advanced swimmers to allow full use of a strong chest and shoulder muscles. However, in the early stages of learning, the body should remain as stable as possible.

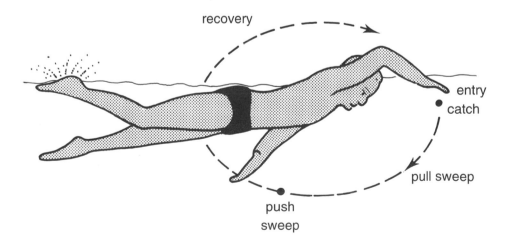

Figure 7.5 *The front-crawl stroke, showing high elbow recovery and fingertips entering the water first*

Leg action

The main function of the *leg kick* is to stabilise the body, keeping it balanced, but the legs also maintain the body position and give some forward propulsion. The leg kick is alternating and is initiated from the hips. The legs swing up and down in the vertical plane within the body depth.

The *downkick* begins at the hip. The knee, slightly bent at commencement, is straightened during the downkick. The foot is extended throughout (*plantar-flexed*), and where there is good ankle flexibility, in-toeing will result. The downkick is an accelerating, whip-like action. During the upkick, the sole of the extended foot and the back of the leg press upwards and backwards against the water. There is a slight bending of the knee as the leg moves towards the surface. At the end of the upkick, the heels should just break the water surface.

Arm action

The main function of the arms is to propel the body, and in order to obtain maximum propulsion from them, it is very important that the alternating movement be continuous and that one arm or the other always be engaged in the *underwater pull*.

Entry

The hand enters the water in advance of the head at a point between the nose and the shoulder line on its own side. The elbow is flexed and raised, and the forearm slopes downwards to the hand which is stretched out firmly and pitched slightly outwards so that the thumb and first finger enter the water first. The hand enters the water first, followed by the wrist and then the elbow which remains high.

Catch

As soon as the hand has entered the water, it slides forward, remaining close to the surface. Once it reaches almost full stretch, it presses down and slightly out and 'catches' the water. The hand now sweeps *downwards* and the elbow starts to flex, which allows the hand to keep a hold on the water.

Insweep

At the end of the downsweep, the elbow flexes more and the pitch of the hand turns inwards towards the midline of the body. Elbow flexion continues to increase until it reaches approximately 90 degrees, bringing the hand in to the midline of the body. The hand is accelerating throughout this part of the arm pull.

Upsweep

The pitch of the hand changes again so that it faces backwards and outwards. Throughout this stage, the fingers stay pointing to the bottom of the pool. Only at the end of the upsweep does the hand release and rotate so that the little finger is ready at the surface to follow the elbow into the recovery. The upsweep should take the hand right through to the hips. The arm, at the end of the upsweep, should be almost fully extended.

Recovery

The elbow clears the water first, followed by the hand, little finger first. The arm is carried forward over the water surface to the entry point, keeping as close to the midline as possible. A low swinging recovery will cause the hips to swing laterally and should therefore be avoided. The recovery should occur in a relaxed manner.

Breathing

It is important that breathing interfere with the rhythm of the stroke as little as possible, so timing the *inbreath* accurately is vital. The pupil should focus on rolling the head sideways and not lifting it. The pupil can breathe to one side *unilaterally* or to alternate sides ever one and a half stroke cycles – *bilaterally*.

There are two methods of breathing in the front crawl stroke: *explosive* or *trickle* breathing.

Explosive breathing (see Figure 7.6) is used by the swimmer under pressure: either the nervous beginner or a competitive swimmer. The breath is held for most of the underwater armstroke, and air is then forced out towards the end of the upsweep. Then, when the mouth clears the water at the start of the recovery phase, there is a short phase of inhalation.

A more leisurely method of breathing is trickle breathing (see Figure 7.7). Here, the breath is gently exhaled through the mouth and nose during the whole underwater armstroke of the arm on the breathing side. Inhalation takes place when the mouth has cleared the water as the arm on the breathing side lifts at the start of recovery.

Initially, it is best to use trickle breathing unilaterally as the pupils experience a longer phase of exhalation and inhalation than in explosive breathing. Pupils need to understand the importance of exhaling at the correct time in the stroke cycle.

(a)

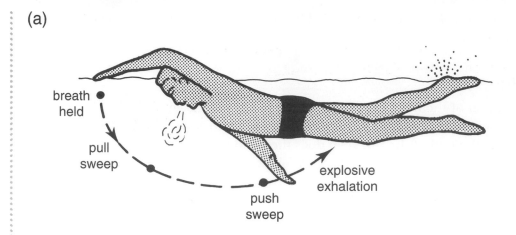

(b)

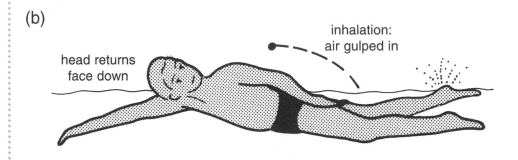

Figure 7.6 (a) (b) *Explosive breathing in the front crawl*

(a)

(b)

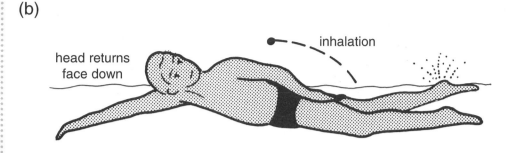

Figure 7.7 (a) (b) *Trickle breathing in the front crawl*

Timing

Usually, there are six beats of the legs to one complete arm cycle. The rhythm should be continuous and smooth, and the stroke should look flowing. The leg action should create a steady regular small splash, with the heels just breaking the water surface.

Table 7.3 *Causes and corrections for faults in the front crawl*

Fault: Head too high out of water
Cause: Fear of putting face in the water
              Lack of understanding
              Incorrect breathing technique
Correction: Return to early confidence work if required
              Further stroke practice, with emphasis on face in the water
              Reteach correct breathing technique

Fault: Legs too low in the water
Cause: Weak leg kick
              Lack of understanding about the need for streamlining
Correction: Push and glide
              Early leg practices emphasising heels up to surface

Fault: Excessive knee bending
Cause: Lack of understanding of correct technique
Correction: Leg practices with emphasis on long, loose legs. Swing from the hips

Fault: Body 'snakes' through the water
Cause: Entry position of hand is across the midline
              Limb track underwater is incorrect

Correction: Reteach correct hand entry position – between nose and shoulder, in advance of the head on its own side
Practice arm action standing. Check pathway of pulling arm

Fault: Dropped elbow during arm pull
Cause: Lack of knowledge of correct technique
Correction: Arm practices, emphasising 'high' elbow during propulsive phase

Fault: Wide recovery
Cause: Lack of flexibility in shoulders
Lack of understanding
Correction: Land exercises to improve shoulder flexibility
Reteach arm recovery – emphasise high elbow, hand passes close to ear

Fault: Not breathing at all
Cause: Lack of understanding about when to breathe
Correction: Reteach breathing action and the timing of breathing with the arm action

Fault: Breathing at the incorrect time in the stroke cycle
Cause: Lack of knowledge of correct technique
Correction: Reteach when to breathe in relation to the arm action

Table 7.4 *Teaching the front crawl – suggested progressions*

Material	Teaching points	Organisation
1 Push and glide	Let go with the hands Squeeze elbows into sides Arms skim along the water surface – 'Imagine you are sliding across the top of a polished table' Face in the water, keep eyes open Keep ears squeezed between the arms Glide with arms and legs extended and together	Hands hold trough or poolside firmly Feet apart and placed firmly on the wall Spaced out for widthways work

Material	Teaching points	Organisation
2 a) Leg kick at the side of the pool	Hands hold poolside – shoulder-width apart, elbows pressed into the wall Rail undergrasped, trough overgrasped Legs together and near the surface Kick from the hips, long stretched legs Flipper feet Legs swing close together Heels make small rhythmic splash Depth of kick 30–45 cm	Hands hold poolside
b) Leg kick with one or two floats	Grip of floats – 2 floats can be held side by side at the far end with extended arms, or elbows bent so that floats are held knuckle to knuckle	Make sure enough floats are in place on poolside to ensure 2 per pupil
c) Leg kick with arms extended This practice shows the true efficiency of the leg kick	Thumbs locked, arms extended Face in the water, ears squeezed between the arms Body stretched	Widths
3 Dog paddle	Ask question: 'Do you know how a dog swims?' Keep head steady – 'balance a book on your head' 'Blow as you go!' Keep arms in the water, hands firm Slide arm forwards as far as you can Pull firmly, fingers together, elbow slightly bent Pull, then push back until the thumb touches the thigh, then bend elbow and slide arm forward along the side of the body to start again Keep leg kick going as before	Widths

Material	Teaching points	Organisation
4 Arm action, standing	Pupils stand knees bent, feet apart, leading forwards so that shoulders are in the water Hands firm, fingers together, tips of fingers enter the water first Elbow raised Entry between nose and shoulder Hold hand and elbow firmly at 'catch' point Hand stays close to body midline as it passes back Thumb brushes thigh Lift elbow from the water first for recovery Carry hand forwards close to the side of the body to entry point again Keep action flowing and rhythmic	Pupils stand spread out in shallow water
5 Co-ordinate the whole stroke	a) Push and glide, then bring in leg kick b) Then push and glide + leg kick + the arm action. (Hold breath.) Teaching points as appropriate for each phase of the stroke Maintain a steady rhythm	Widthways
6 a) Breathing, standing	Standing – lean forwards, one foot in front of the other, shoulders and face in the water Concentrate on rolling the head to the side Think about: nose in the water, ear in the water Practice blowing out into the water through the mouth and nose Keep exhaling as the head is rolled to the side When mouth is clear of the water, breathe in; close your mouth before rolling the head back Try to get a smooth breathing rhythm	Pupils stand in shallow water, spread out and spaced well so that when they roll their heads they are not looking directly at their neighbour

Material	Teaching points	Organisation
b) Leg kick + float + breathing	Blow out firmly as head is rolled into the space made by the bent arm on the breathing side, and work on the *flow* of the head roll	Widthways One float per pupil (The float is held by the arm on the breathing side at the near end, the non-breathing arm at the far end)
7 Arm action + breathing	Stand feet apart, knees bent, shoulders in the water; lean forwards Decide on the breathing side As hand on breathing side enters water, blow firmly through nose and mouth Keep face in the water and blow out until the pulling arm passes under the nose Still blowing out, roll the head to the side Breathe in as the mouth clears the water; this usually coincides with the breathing-arm elbow clearing the water Close the mouth and return the face to the water as the breathing arm passes the face during the recovery; repeat	Pupils spread out in shallow water
8 Co-ordinate the whole stroke	a) Push and glide, bring in leg kick, arm action but no breathing b) Repeat, but take one breath halfway across the width c) Gradually increase the number of breaths taken	Widthways

It is recommended that only one teaching point be emphasised at a time.

► BREASTSTROKE

The *breaststroke* is a popular stroke for many beginners, mainly because the head is raised naturally, making breathing easy. The swimmer can also see where they are going, and it is ideal as a survival/social stroke, with most of the limb movements underwater. It is, however, the slowest of the four major strokes as it is least streamlined with the lower hip position.

There have been many changes in the teaching of the breaststroke, mainly in the leg action. The narrower 'whip kick' which has been developed for many years is streamlined and very effective propulsively. The Amateur Swimming Association (ASA) law is very strict, and states that 'after the completion of the start and turn from the beginning of the first arm stroke, the body shall be kept on the breast and both shoulders shall be in line with the normal water surface ... All movements of the arms and feet shall be simultaneous and in the same horizontal plane without alternating movement' (Amateur Swimming Association, 1997).

Body position

The body is as stretched as possible, but there is a slope to the hips to enable the leg action to take place without breaking the surface of the water. The hips are usually 15–20 cm underwater. The head should be as steady as possible, with the face clear of the water, and the waterline just fractionally above or below the mouth.

Leg action

There are two main leg kicks in the breaststroke: the *whip kick* (see Figure 7.8) and the *wedge kick* (see Figure 7.9). The whip kick is preferable from the point of view of propulsion and streamlining, but it requires greater knee and ankle mobility. The wedge kick is valuable for those lacking knee-joint mobility – the disabled swimmer, for example, is often more successful using the wedge kick.

The whip kick is often described in three phases: *bend, turn* and *drive*.

1   *Bend* – the legs and feet commence from an extended position (close together). The feet are drawn up towards the seat by bending and parting the knees and thighs until they are slightly wider apart than hip width. The angle between the trunk and thigh at this point is never less than 90 degrees. The feet during this phase are sole-uppermost, with toes pointing backwards, and they part a few inches as they travel towards the seat. They are *dorsiflexed* (flattened), with the toes still pointing backwards during the latter part of the bend.

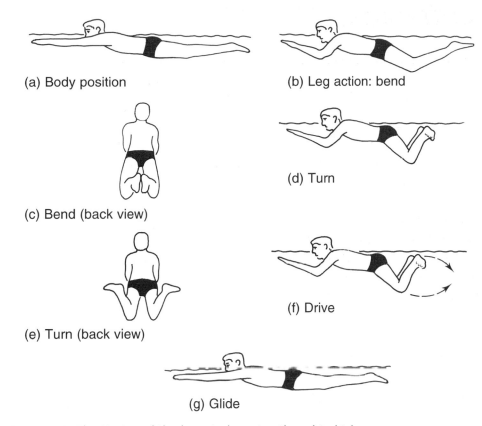

(a) Body position

(b) Leg action: bend

(c) Bend (back view)

(d) Turn

(e) Turn (back view)

(f) Drive

(g) Glide

Figure 7.8 *The timing of the breaststroke using the whip kick*

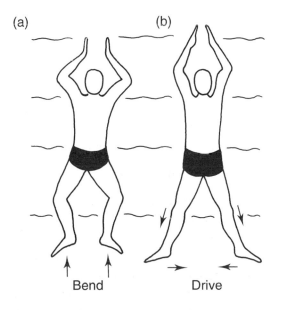

(a)

(b)

Bend

Drive

Figure 7.9 *The wedge kick for the breaststroke*

2   *Turn* – this part of the kick is essential to its success as it enables the inner border of the lower legs and feet to prepare for the drive back against the water. The feet in the dorsiflexed position are *everted* – i.e. cocked outwards – and the soles are still facing uppermost. The inner border of the feet and lower leg present a useful surface for driving backwards.

3   *Drive* – the feet, still everted and dorsiflexed, commence the backward drive, and the path is backwards and slightly outwards. The swimmer should concentrate on the *heels'* drawing a somewhat circular pattern as they travel backwards. The narrower kick is more efficient than a wide kick.

    The speed of the kick is important. The feet should increase speed on the drive back so that they snap together with the soles uppermost. The feet and legs should be extended and together on completion of the drive. The feet rise slightly at this point. The length of glide is dependent on the efficiency of the kick and on whether the swimmer is a competitive or recreational swimmer. A beginner should be encouraged to work towards a short glide, whereas in a competitive swimmer this is minimal.

The whip kick is the most popular kick now, but it must be taught with great care as once a fault develops it is extremely difficult to correct.

The wedge kick is described because some beginners often find it easier to learn: adults and many less mobile swimmers often prefer a more angular leg action, finding it less stressful on the knee joints than the whip kick.

The wedge kick can be described in two phases: *bend* and *drive*.

1   *Bend* – the knees are bent outwards and the heels kept together, with the soles of the feet facing backwards. The legs are in a diamond position at this point, with an approximately 90 degree angle between the trunk and thighs.

2   *Drive* – the legs start to kick outwards, with the soles of the feet pressing against the water. When the legs have extended, they are squeezed into a stretched 'glide' position.

Arm action

The *arm action* can be described under two headings: the *propulsive phase* (out, down and in sweeps) and the *recovery phase* (arms stretch into glide).

1   *Propulsive phase:*

   ● *Outward sweep* – in the extended glide position where the arms, hands and fingers are together, and the palms face downwards under the water surface, the hands are now angled/pitched palms slightly outwards, with little finger higher than thumb. The arms are straight at this point and sweep outwards and slightly downwards to the catch position shoulder-width apart.

- *Downsweep* – the sweep continues downward and slightly outwards and the elbows bending, remain high. (I say to the pupils that the arms should look like a coat hanger!) The arms should reach a point to the side and level with the shoulders.

- *Insweep* – the insweep really commences just before shoulder level. The upper arms begin to squeeze to the sides of the body, palms pitched slightly inwards as if moving to a praying position. The elbows also close to the sides. The latter part of the insweep increases pace.

2 *Recovery phase:* the arms are extended forwards in front of the body. There should be a slight glide before the next pull commences. (The glide will be possible to achieve if the leg kick has been effective. The glide is not desirable for a competitive swimmer.)

Breathing

Breathing can again be trickle or explosive. It is usually taken every cycle. Explosive breathing is commonly used by competitive swimmers. Trickle breathing is preferable for the beginner and is comparatively easy to teach as the face is usually kept clear of water. As the arms commence their pull, the body is lifted slightly and inhalation takes place through the nose and mouth. At the end of the pull sweep, to coincide with the arm and leg bend, the mouth is shut. Exhalation occurs as the arms extend forward in the glide and the legs drive back. A more able swimmer usually adopts explosive breathing. They are under pressure during the pull sweep, so the breath is automatically held. At the end of the pull sweep, the head is lifted/raised and the trunk is higher in the water. Air is forced out through the nose and mouth, and an inbreath immediately follows as the arms squeeze to the sides. The mouth is then closed and the arms stretch forwards.

Timing

The arms and legs are together in the glide or extended position. The arms pull, and the legs remain extended. The elbows are tucked to the side with hands under the chin, and at the same time, the legs bend. The feet are turned outwards (everted) and drive backwards while the arms extend forward into the glide position. This position should be held for a short time before the cycle commences. Inhalation for beginners takes place on the pull, exhalation on the glide.

Table 7.5 *Causes and corrections for faults in the breaststroke*

	Fault	Cause	Correction
Body position	Bobbing	Head too high – fear? Directing kick down and not back	Return to confidence work and early stages of breaststroke
	Head high, low hips	Fear	As for bobbing
Legs	Feet not everting and dorsiflexing	Lack of understanding Stiff ankles	Return to early leg work
	Screw or uneven kick	Breathing to side Knee-joint problem Swimming side-stroke	Leg work Concentrate on knees together on leg bend and on the symmetry of *bend, turn feet and drive back*
Arms	Pulling too far back	Weak legs	Work on leg kick generally
	Short and shallow pull	Lack of understanding	Return to recheck arm practices and co-ordination
Breathing	Breathing to the side	Fear, lack of confidence and understanding	Reteach basics and confidence work
	Head held too high for breathing	Fear	Return to basics and confidence work
Timing	Non-stop arm action	Weak legs	Return to basics and confidence work
	Not extending arms and legs into glide	Lack of understanding	Return to early practices

NB: only a few faults listed for this stroke.

Table 7.6 *Teaching the breaststroke – suggested progressions*

Material	Teaching points	Organisation
1 Push and glide from the poolside (How far can the pupil travel?)	Release hands from rail Squeeze elbows to sides Drive off with legs Arms slide along the water surface ('Imagine you are sliding along the top of a polished table') Face in water, eyes open	Spaced out by side Grip rail/trough, feet apart on wall
2 Leg kick at rail or trough (time must be taken to ensure the leg kick is correct)	Grip trough firmly, elbows press into wall Shoulders and trunk symmetrical Legs together and feet stretched in glide position. Soles uppermost. Work on *ankle mobility* (See diagram:) a) stretch and curl feet b) turn feet east and west stretch and curl feet, and then add turn east and west *Work on bend part of leg action:* Knees: bend just outside hip width Feet: soles uppermost, parted slightly and dorsiflexed *Turning the feet:* Now join this vital part of the stroke to the bend. Turning or everting the feet should ensure the insides of the feet and lower leg are ready to drive back Repeat from the extended legs to bend, and add *back drive*. Heels play a major role in narrow backward drive circular movements. The kick should increase speed until feet snap together, soles uppermost	Spaced out at poolside. For any child not able to cope with holding the side whilst they work on the leg action, have a few armbands available and thread some string through each. Tie an armband to the hip – this provides support whilst the pupil works on angle mobility
3 a) Leg kick, holding two floats	a) Check grip on floats (arms can be extended and hold far end of float, or elbows can be placed on float and held at 90 degree angle with hands knuckle to knuckle)	Working widthways 2 floats (check grip of floats)

Material	Teaching points	Organisation
	Teaching points as for (2). When feet are together and legs extended in glide, count two before commencing again (this discourages a rushed movement) Check kick is symmetrical	
b) Leg kick, holding one float	Teaching points as above. Work to reduce number of leg kicks per width. An indication of a more efficient movement	Widthways One float
c) Leg kick, arms extended	Arms stretched Thumbs locked Chin resting on water surface	Widthways
4 a) Arm action, standing in shallow end	Lean forward, shoulders in water. Feet astride hip width, heels down, knees bend, arms in extended position	Pupils spread out. Check stance in shallow end
i) Out and down sweep	From the extended arm position, the arms move downwards and then back and downwards in a sweeping movement. They reach a point just in front of the shoulder line and should then tuck to the side	
ii) Insweep	Elbows tuck speedily to the side, palms of the hands in the praying position	
iii) Glide or stretch	Glide or stretch forwards underwater	
b) Arm action, walking	Teaching points as for 4a	Shoulders should be kept beneath the water surface
5 Arm action and breathing	i) Pull sweep, breathe in. ii) As arms and legs tuck, close mouth. iii) As arms extend into glide 'blow the hands forward'	

Material	Teaching points	Organisation
6 a) Co-ordinating the stroke	i) Arms sweep ii) Elbows tuck to side and one leg bends iii) Arms extend into glide beyond the head as leg kick snaps back	Teacher demonstrates co-ordinated stroke, standing on bathside in an upright position
b) Working on the co-ordinated stroke	Work to cut down number of strokes. Include a small glide	Children swim widths building up whole stroke

THE INVERTED BREASTSTROKE

It is often useful to be able to use a breaststroke leg action in the *supine* position. If pupils have a problem learning breaststroke in the prone position, they may well find it useful to start on their backs where they can watch their feet and concentrate on the relevant foot movements. This approach can be used to help correct an asymmetrical or screw kick. Many disabled swimmers can cope with this kick and combine it with a scull to make a stroke in which the arm and leg movements are kept in the water, which is good for buoyancy and stability. It is also an invaluable kick in life-saving or personal survival.

The body position

There is usually a downward slope to the hips. The head is raised slightly, with eyes looking at the feet or at an angle of 45 degrees. The sloping body ensures that the leg movement is in the water.

Leg action

The leg action (see Figure 7.10) is very similar to the breaststroke kick. The legs are used to propel, balance and maintain the body position, and, as in the breaststroke, the feet are important if the kick is to be effective: they should preferably be dorsiflexed throughout the kick.

The kick can be described in three phases: the *bend*, the *turn of the feet* and the *kick*.

1 *Bend* – the body slopes from the hips to the knees. The hips should not bend much since the movement comes mainly from the lower leg. The

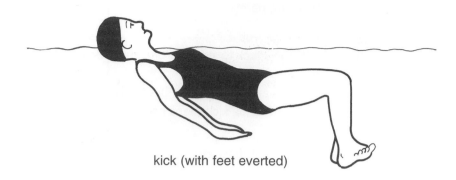

kick (with feet everted)

Figure 7.10 *Leg action in the inverted breaststroke*

lower legs, with the feet dorsiflexed, drop from the knee so that there is an angle between the calf and thigh of almost 90 degrees. The heels and knees should be approximately hip-width apart at this stage.

2   *Turn* – the feet evert so that the inside of the lower leg and foot is ready to press against the water during the kick, exactly as in the breaststroke.

3   *Kick* – made by a drive slightly outwards but mainly backwards, with the inner border of the feet and lower legs pressing hard against the water and the *heels* drawing a circular pattern. The feet should come together on completion.

Arm action

The arms can scull by the side of the body (see Figure 7.11(a), remain in the water and sweep sideways from the thigh to an extended position at the side of the shoulders before sweeping back towards the thigh (see Figure 7.11(b), or be lifted clear of the water simultaneously in a double back crawl arm action. I would suggest that in primary schools the first two methods are the best combination with the leg kick:

- Method 1: *sculling using the standard or head-first method of travel.*
- Method 2: *the sweeping movement.* The extended arms are by the thighs. They are both swept sideways, with the palm of the hand downwards and the little finger leading the way to a position to the side of and level with the shoulders. The thumbs are turned upwards so that the palm of the hand is similar to a paddle. The fingers should be together, arm and hands held firmly. The arm is pressed down into the water a little before following a semi-circular sweep to reach the thighs. The palms of the hands reach the thighs, and the movement is repeated.

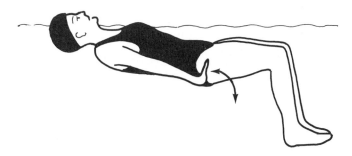

(a) Standard scull

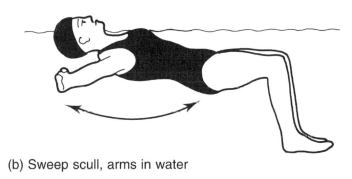

(b) Sweep scull, arms in water

Figure 7.11 *Types of arm action in the inverted breaststroke*

Breathing

One advantage of this stroke is that breathing is easy. It can just be kept going naturally or, if possible, fitted into the stroke. I usually tell pupils to time their breathing with the kick: 'As the knees bend breathe in, and as the legs kick, blow out.'

Timing

If the sweeping arm movement is used, the arms should extend from the thighs sideways as the legs bend to 90 degrees. The kick follows and the arms sweep underwater to the thighs. If a head-first or standard scull is used, the sculling action must be as *continuous* and rhythmic as possible, and the leg action is executed as described.

THE DOLPHIN BUTTERFLY STROKE

The dolphin butterfly is the fourth major competitive stroke to be recognised, and it is the second fastest stroke after the front crawl.

The dolphin butterfly as we know it today is a stroke requiring strength, flexibility and general watermanship. The teacher often excludes it because it might be too demanding or because of uncertainty about how to teach it. I introduce only the kick to children to start with, and they invariably love the fish-like movements both on and under the water surface. Once they have confidence in this, they can develop a long narrow breaststroke-type arm action and co-ordinate it with a dolphin kick. If the entire movement is kept *in* the water, it is not so demanding. When the children become stronger, they can learn the over-arm recovery. For the majority of upper primary children, correctly timed two-beat dolphin kick, combined with an underwater arm action, is adequate and far more beneficial than an overwater movement which is invariably incorrectly executed.

This is an easy stroke to teach if the teacher follows the steps suggested, although there are teachers who might introduce it by concentrating on an arm action and letting the legs react to the arm movements. Whether one emphasises legs or arms in the early stages, I hope this stroke will be considered in all timetables.

The body position

The body position in the dolphin butterfly stroke is similar in many ways to that for the front crawl stroke. The water level initially should cut the crown of the head but will vary from person to person according to physical factors. The body should be as horizontal as possible, with shoulders kept level, but there should be a slope to the legs so that most of the leg kick is in the water.

The undulating body action in this stroke should be kept to a minimum. It will vary according to strength and flexibility.

Leg action

The leg action helps to keep the body flat, aids propulsion a little and helps the swimmer to cope with breathing by supporting the body. An efficient leg action also helps the continuity and effectiveness of the underwater arm pull and balances the arm action.

1st kick

start of
first kick

2nd kick

start of
second kick

Figure 7.12 *The timing of leg and arm action in the dolphin butterfly stroke*

The leg action is simultaneous and is initiated from the hip. The depth of the kick will range from a flutter, 'tadpole' type of movement to a kick which can be deeper than the body depth. If the kick is too deep, however, the hips will rise and a porpoising, excessively undulating stroke will develop.

The leg action starts at the hip: a downward kick commences with the legs slightly bent at the surface. The feet move downwards vigorously. The knees come closer together and straighten at the same time. The hips rise slightly.

The upward kick starts from the trailing leg position. Both legs, with the feet together, move upwards, and the knees bend and will often part slightly as the feet are nearing the surface. An in-toeing effect is often seen if the knees are parted slightly during the upward movement. (NB: the swimmer should endeavour to keep the feet together throughout the kick.)

Arm action

The arms mainly propel the body, and if they are to work effectively, strength and shoulder flexibility are advantages. The arm action can be described under the headings of *entry, propelling sweeps* and *recovery*.

1   *Entry* – the hands enter the water in advance of the head, with elbows raised slightly. There should be a slight downward slope from the elbows to

the hands. The hand entry for beginners could be fingertips first and fingers together. With more able swimmers, the hand entry should be pitched (angled) slightly out, thumb first and fingers together.

The position of entry can range from opposite the nose to slightly wider than shoulder width. Initially, entry between the nose and the shoulder line is preferable. With weaker swimmers, slightly wider entry might enable them to cope with a V-shaped backward sweep better than would a more central entry where the hands might slip outwards and miss the downward and inward sweeps.

2 *Propelling sweeps* – the keyhole pattern is described in the *underwater* arm sweeps. *Outward (pitch) sweep:* following the entry, the hands, stretched out flat sweep out and slightly *downwards* to *catch*. *Downward* pressure continues with the elbows bending, and the coathanger effect (as in the breaststroke) is seen, with high bent elbows and lower hands. The arms are now just outside/level with the shoulder line. (So far, the circular part of the keyhole has been described.) *In, back and up sweeps:* the swimmers would find it easier to follow this if they are told to turn the hands *inwards* – palms back, thumb knuckles up, elbows still high. The hands often meet and then press *back* under the centre of the body. (This completes the narrow part of the keyhole.) As the arms sweep under the body, the speed of movement is accelerated and the elbows are almost straightened. The thumbs can brush the hips, followed by the slightly bent elbows being lifted from the water, followed by the hands – little finger uppermost.

3 *Recovery* – the shoulders and upper arms are slightly lifted so that the elbows can lift clear of the water, the little finger clearing the water first. The arms rotate as they swing over the water in the low swinging recovery. They should be almost straight. The recovery resembles a low arc clearing the water surface. The arms must clear the water surface to comply with ASA law.

NB: as soon as the arms complete recovery, they should re-enter the water into the next arm cycle without pause.

Breathing

The swimmer can breathe forwards or to the side, but if side breathing is used the swimmer must make sure the shoulders remain symmetrical. Side breathing can help to maintain a flatter body position. Forward breathing is more popular. Whichever position the swimmer chooses to breathe in, it must be timed correctly with the arm cycle and leg kick. A flexible neck is an advantage.

Breathing is explosive and late in this stroke. The exhalation through the nose and mouth commences during the latter part of underwater pull sweep as the hands are passing underneath the nose and travelling towards the hips. The second beat of a two-beat dolphin stroke coincides with the start of exhalation. The head is then lowered, or in side breathing rotated, back to fact into the water as the arms are swinging in the low recovery.

Alternate breathing, i.e. breathing every other cycle, helps the body to keep a flatter position.

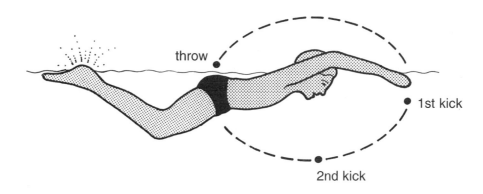

Figure 7.13 *Timing in the dolphin butterfly stroke*

Timing

Continuity of the arm action is necessary if the stroke is to be executed well. The stroke can have a one- or two-beat kick to each arm cycle, but it is preferable in teaching to have a two-beat kick. The swimmer should time the kicks to coincide with specific points in the arm action (see Figure 7.13). The kicks should be fairly shallow. The first downkick takes place at the start of the underwater arm sweep at *catch point*. This keeps the body flatter. The second beat is usually towards the end of the inward sweep as the arms are pressing backwards and passing under the nose. The second beat gives the body position a final lift for the latter part of the final upward sweep when exhalation commences, and prevents the body from being lowered and rolled unduly as the head is raised or rolled to the side for inhalation. The kicks are not always of the same strength: often, the second beat is lighter. This heavy-beat–light-beat sequence is called *major–minor kick*. (Some competitive swimmers deliberately reverse the procedure, making the minor kick the more important as they prefer the body to lift as the arms are clearing the water to recovery.)

Table 7.7 *Causes and corrections for faults in the butterfly dolphin*

	Fault	Cause	Correction
Body position	Too much undulation	Kicking down too deeply on first beat 'Diving' into arm entry Raising and lowering head too much for breathing	Return to leg stroke practices and progress through stages
	Body too angled	Weak legs. Head too high for breathing	Work on legs and general stroke streamlining
Legs	Too great a knee bend	Lack of strength Lack of understanding	Return to reteach leg kick
	Kick out of water	Lack of strength Lack of understanding	Return to leg kick
Arms	Collapsing elbow on arm entry	Weak arms. Lack of strength	Work on building up arms and general strength
	Feathering/ slipping at catch point, and arms leave water too early	Lack of shoulder/arm strength	Return to reteach arms
Breathing	Lifting body and trunk too high for breathing	Lack of leg-kick strength	Return to build up legs
	Not breathing	Fear Lack of understanding Concentration	Confidence and breathing practices
Timing	Pausing on arm entry	Weakness and lack of strength	Recheck stages and build strength
	Both legs kick too close together, i.e. just after entry	Lack of understanding of timing Lack of strength	Rebuild stroke and revise correct timing. Build strength

NB: only a few faults listed for this stroke.

Table 7.8 *Teaching the dolphin butterfly stroke – suggested progressions*

Material	Teaching points	Organisation
1 a) Push and glide along the water surface	Release hands from rail Squeeze elbows to sides Drive off legs, arms slide along surface ('imagine you are sliding along the top of a polished table') Head between arms, face in water, eyes open	Spread out, backs to wall Working widthways, swimmers could work in 2s. Check one another – for example, on a technical point given by the teacher
b) Sink, push and glide underwater	Blow out while submerging. Push off hard and glide. Body streamlined, arms extended, head squeezed between arms, nose down, eyes open. Work for distance	Stand with backs to wall Sink with back vertical, and sit on heels Rotate onto front, nose down and place feet on wall
2 Leg kick at rail or trough	The lower legs kick together. Thighs remain steady and in line diagonally with trunk Hips 20–30 cm underwater Small splash should be seen, feet just breaking water surface	Under grip rail or over trough, arms shoulder width apart
3 Push and glide underwater and add leg kick	Start leg kick underwater on front, then roll onto side and back, still kicking Work on a small kick, mainly from the knee, in a steady rhythm	As for 1b
4 Leg kick, holding one or two floats. Leg practice holding a float should be limited NB: due to the stress to the lower back when holding a float	Head up for this activity Chin on the water surface Leg kick as described (Grip floats firmly top end of float)	Widthways or lengthways Floats spread along poolside by each pupil
5 Leg kick with arms extended at the water surface	Leg kick as above Blow *out* frequently	

Material	Teaching points	Organisation
6 a) Long, narrow underwater breaststroke arm action, standing in shallow end	Lean forwards Pupils work for long, narrow pull Arms commence from breaststroke glide position	Standing in the shallow end, shoulders underwater
b) Long, narrow breaststroke pull, walking	Arms firmly held, move slightly outwards and mainly back Raise elbows during insweep by turning upper arms inwards Continue sweep well past shoulders Touch hips Tuck elbows to side of body speedily by rotating upper arm outwards Extend arms forwards	
7 Arm action only	As for 6. Chin up, body slanting slightly downwards	Swim widths
8 Co-ordinate arm action and leg kick Add 2 dolphin leg kicks	Chin up, body slanting Commence long, breaststroke arm action Encourage an even rhythm First kick as arm pull commences, second kick as arms pass under nose. Work for continuity The full stroke rhythm should be kick, stretch arms forwards underwater	
9 Add breathing	Blow out as second kick starts and arms pass nose Lift head but not shoulders (stress neck mobility) Breathe in as arms tuck to sides	Swim widths
(NB: at this point, most primary children have had enough of the stroke until they are stronger. I would only add the over-water recovery for older children.)		
10 a) Overwater arm action, standing in shallow end	Hands enter water, between nose and shoulder line Elbows raised, wrists firmly held Draw keyhole pattern	Standing position in shallow end as for breaststroke arm action 6a

Material	Teaching points	Organisation
b) Over-water recovery – walking in shallow end	When arms are by hips, upper arm clears water, then lower arm, with little finger leading Swing arms forward to entry point Repeat Continuity is essential Head steady, face in water	
11 Co-ordinate complete stroke Bring in over-water arm action and add two dolphin leg kicks	No breathing yet First kick at start of pull Second kick as hands travel back underwater passing nose Work for continuity and unbroken rhythm. No glide after recovery	Swim widths
12 Add breathing	Stress blowing out on the second beat and lifting head right back Work for continuity of stroke during breathing, adding one good breath halfway across the pool and breathholding the remainder. Work up to breathing every stroke or every other stroke.	Swim widths
13 Rhythm	Rhythm essential first kick second kick arm throw | | | head down blow out return head raise head	

General stroke analysis

As already pointed out, a good teacher must observe their pupils to decide how best to guide them. With experience it becomes second nature to follow a specific format. You will need to recognise BLABT:

B = Body Position
L = Leg Action
A = Arm Action
B = Breathing
T = Timing/Co-ordination

You will need to look at *each* of the above factors from various angles, i.e. above (if possible), sideways, coming towards you and going away. Your analysis should identify both good and bad features, and a very detailed analysis should give a very clear picture of the stroke. It is helpful if you imagine describing over a telephone the stroke you are analysing.

Frequently, teachers can locate a fault, and the important thing then is to decide on the *cause* and *treat it*. The majority of teachers can find a fault, but recognition of the cause will only develop with experience. Let us look at a few examples. A breaststroke swimmer pulls non-stop on arm action, and the teacher endeavours to teach a short glide. Invariably, the pupil is just trying to survive! The leg action is usually poor, and they are having to rely on the arm action to keep the body up and to propel. In the back crawl, a pause in the arm pull or scull by the hips is a sign of weak legs. A pause/rest just after arm entry on the dolphin butterfly indicates using leg power inadequately and mistiming leg beats. If the front crawl appears rhythmical when you are viewing it, check the swimmer is breathing! If the stroke then still flows, this is ideal.

Important: if you are writing a detailed analysis, ask the swimmer to do a couple of widths/lengths and then pause for a breather before continuing, otherwise the stroke deteriorates and your analysis becomes inaccurate.

The teacher plan for stroke analysis could be as follows. The teacher must *observe* to gain a general impression of the *whole* stroke. Does the stroke look rhythmical/flow? If it flows, there is usually no major problem. There should be economy of effort in an efficient stroke. The body streamlining for the stroke should be ideal for the stroke being executed, and breathing should fit into the cycle without disturbing the rhythm. The following tabulated points the teacher can observe initially. They can affect the component parts of the stroke:

1 *Body position:*

(i) *Fear* of water.

(ii) *Head*

– too high;
– too low;
– movement within stroke performance.

(iii) *Shoulder*

– position in water;
– shoulder movement within stroke performance;
– shoulder symmetry when necessary, e.g. breaststroke.

(iv) *Hip*

– position in water;
– movement within stroke performance.

(v) *Leg*

– kick in relation to water surface;
– movement within stroke performance.

(vi) *Arm*

– action can affect the body position;
– check entry *point*, e.g. over centre line in a front crawl will cause a *longitudinal roll*;
– too flat an arm entry on a front crawl will cause a *vertical bob*;
– recovery swing, if too wide, will lead to a *lateral* swing.

(vii) *Strength* of the swimmer – e.g. a strong swimmer often leans into the stroke, causing a body roll.

(viii) *Flexibility*. The more shoulder flexibility the better, as the body is usually flatter – e.g. the back-crawl swimmer with flexible shoulders can avoid a body roll in the early stages of learning the stroke.

(ix) *The build* of the swimmer. This relates to hip position too – the buoyant swimmer rides high in the hip area.

(x)   *The speed* of the swimmer. There is usually a higher body position in a swimmer travelling at speed.

2 *Leg action:*

(i)   What is the *function* of the leg kick? Does it propel, stabilise the stroke, maintain body position?

(ii)   Where is the kick *initiated* from?

(iii) *Depth* of the kick – consider the length of the swimmer here.

(iv)   *Height* of the kick.

(v)   *Width* of the kick.

(vi)   *Flexibility* of the ankles.

(vii) *Rhythm* of the kick – is the kick constant like a motor boat, e.g. the crawl stroke? Or is there a slower–fast phase, e.g. as the legs bend on the breast stroke, the movement is slower than the kick back where the pace increases?

3 *Arm action:*

(i)   What is the *function* of the arm action? The arms should propel the body, but they can balance the body too and facilitate the breathing phase of the stroke.

(ii)   *Entry* – following over-water recovery. Check firmness of wrist position of hand, e.g. thumb in palm and entry point in relation to shoulder width, angle of arm on entry and distance in relation to head.

(iii) *The propelling-phase limb track* – what are the paths followed by the hand and arm? Is the arm bent or straight? Are the hand, wrist and elbow held firmly throughout? Is there a change in speed? (E.g. in the front crawl, the underwater sweep increases pace at the last phase of the underwater arm action as the limb moves towards the hip.)

(iv)   *The recovery phase* – when does the recovery commence or finish? What is the position of the hand, arm and elbow at the start of the path followed in recovery? In the over-water recovery, is it high or low (high elbow etc.), wide, narrow, bent or straight? Is the arm recovery rhythmic? (E.g. in the front crawl, if the breath is held, a novice finds the arm recovery easier to keep rhythmic than when they have to fit breathing into the cycle.)

(v)   Generally, are the arms *strong* or *weak*?

(vi)   Are the shoulders *flexible*?

4 *Breathing*

(i)   Does the swimmer understand the *need* to breathe with particular concentration on exhalation?

   (ii)   *Type* of breathing – explosive or a trickle?

   (iii) *When*, during the stroke's *arm* cycle, does exhalation commence/finish and inhalation commence/finish?

   (iv) *Head position* during breathing – lifted or rolling?

   (v) *Stroke rhythm* during breathing – the stroke should flow during the breathing cycle.

5 *Timing*

   (i)   Does the *stroke rhythm* flow? Does breathing fit into the cycle?

   (ii) *How many* leg beats per cycle (for back crawl, front crawl and dolphin butterfly)?

   (iii) Is there a glide in the leg action of the breaststroke? If so, this will indicate that the arms and legs extend together.

(In all strokes, leg action and arm action co-ordinate to make up the stroke cycle. Breathing should fit in so as not to disturb the cycle rhythm.)

▶ STROKE COUNTING

Always keep a check on stroke deterioration. *Stroke counting* will assist here. The teacher tells the pupils to count how many strokes they take for certain lengths, e.g. for the third and sixth lengths they swim. The pupils count the number of times their *arms* complete a stroke cycle for each full length. (A *stroke cycle* is measured from the commencement of the strokes' arm movement to its recommencement.) If the stroke count increases too much, the swimmer may be 'slipping the water', that is, during the underwater phase of the stroke, there is a loss of purchase and 'snatching' of the water.

Table 8.1 *Teacher stroke analysis chart*

Teacher's stroke analysis   BLABT

Swimmer: Stroke

Date:

	Description
1 *General impression:*	

1 *General impression:*
- Rhythmic/flowing
- Confidence – generally minimum effort
- Streamlined
- Breathing confidence

2 *Body position:*
- Fear
- Head position
- Shoulders
- Hips
- Legs
- Arms
- Strength
- Flexibility
- Build
- Speed of stroke

3 *Leg action:*
- Function
  - propel
  - stabilise
  - body position
- Kick initiated from
- Depth
- Height
- Width
- Ankle flexibility
- Rhythm

4 *Arm action:*
- Function
  - propel
  - balance
  - facilitate

- – breathing
- Entry
- Propelling phase
- Recovery phase
- Strong or weak
- Flexible

5 *Breathing:*
- Understanding
- Explosive
- Trickle
- Exhalation
- Inhalation
- Head position
- Stroke rhythm

6 *Timing:*
- Stroke rhythm
- Number of beats per cycle
- Glide
- Co-ordination

ACTION PLAN

Good points:

Problem points:

Table 8.2 *General faults and suggested corrections for strokes*

Fault	Cause	Correction
Body position		
1 Head too high out of water	a Lack of understanding	a Return to early stages of stroke and build up again
	b Fear	b See 3
2 Head too low in the water	Effort to raise the hips Lack of understanding Trying to progress too quickly	Return to body position work and early stages of stroke
3 Fear, leading to body-position faults	Not sufficient guidance in the early stages to overcome fear	Return to confidence activities. Build up slowly
4 Lack of understanding of what is technically correct, leading to body-position faults	Inadequate teaching points and build-up	Revise entire stroke(s), concentrating on basic teaching points
5 Shoulder roll	Lack of flexibility or effort to gain more purchase from water (common with strong-shouldered swimmers). Could also relate to rolling during breathing in prone position, e.g. front-crawl stroke	With a beginner, concentrate on stability of the shoulders, e.g. breathhold on front crawl with slightly wider pull. If the roll relates to a breathing fault, return to the relevant stroke and check the understanding of the technique
6 Asymmetrical shoulders in breaststroke or dolphin butterfly	Bad habit, or pulling more strongly on one arm than the other. Could also be due to side breathing in dolphin butterfly stroke	Return to relevant teaching points of stroke
7 Too buoyant hips, causing them to ride too high in the water	Body build	Adjust head position and strength of leg kick
Leg action		
1 Overkicking and excessive splashing, particularly in front and back crawl	Poor arm propulsion, leading to overuse of legs Lack of understanding	Revise teaching points. Flippers can often help

Fault	Cause	Correction
2 Bending knees too much in front and back crawl	Lack of understanding, or trying too hard ('cycling')	Tighten front thigh muscles, stretch feet and knees, swing from the hip. The teacher will often have to work on these points on the bathside and guide the pupil manually at first, following up immediately with practice in the water
3 Feet not dorsiflexed sufficiently in breaststroke	Poor ankle flexibility. Weak muscles. Lack of understanding	The broom can be used. Return to progressive leg practices and build up
4 Too deep a kick	Lack of understanding	Return to progressive leg practices
5 Too shallow a kick. 'Tadpole kick' in front and back crawl	Weakness Lack of knowledge	Return to early stages of leg action. Flippers can help all strokes except breaststroke
6 Too wide a kick	Too large thighs. Lack of hip mobility. Lack of understanding of the stroke	Check technical knowledge Over-exaggerate narrower legs. Work on leg action generally
7 Asymmetrical kick (breaststroke and dolphin butterfly) and/or a screw kick (breaststroke)	Bad habit. Lazy leg. Anatomical problem at knee and/or hip joint Lack of understanding	Return to rail or trough, then with a float, build up number of kicks. With the screw kick, check that the knees and feet mirror each other on the bend. 'Glue' the knees and feet together at this point; kick and glide should then be *slowly* executed. Patience is required with this correction. Progress to float work for a few kicks and then stop and rest before repeating a few more kicks. Some screw kicks can be corrected by the inverted breaststroke in which the pupil can watch the action

Arm action

Fault	Cause	Correction
1 Lack of flexibility in shoulders		Adjust the stroke to suit the individual, e.g. wider entry in back crawl
2 Crossing over at the centre line at entry in front and back crawl	Lack of understanding	Over-exaggerate a wider entry and return to progressive practices

Fault	Cause	Correction
3 Too wide an entry	Lack of understanding or possible lack of strength	Over-exaggerate a narrower entry and return to progressive practices
4 Wrist, hand, elbow incorrectly held at entry point	Weakness or lack of knowledge	Return to early skills and build up again. In the case of the swimmer with too continuous or rapid a pull, encourage them to decrease the number of strokes taken to cover a set distance
5 Slipping the catch point	Weakness or lack of knowledge	Correction as for 4
6 Too wide a pull	Weakness or lack of knowledge	Correction as for 4
7 Too short a pull	Weakness or lack of knowledge	Correction as for 4
8 Too long a pull in breaststroke	Poor leg kick or lack of knowledge	Work on leg action and progress
9 Pulling across the centre line in the underwater pull in front crawl	Lack of knowledge or weakness or leaning into stroke to use strength	Revise the progressions. Over-exaggerate a wider pull
10 Too wide a recovery in front and back crawl	Poor flexibility. Lack or knowledge	Check teaching points. Emphasise points arm should pass during recovery – e.g. in front crawl, hand and elbow pass close to head
11 Too high a recovery in front crawl	Lack of knowledge	Correction as for 10

Breathing

Fault	Cause	Correction
1 Not breathing at all	Tension – a non-swimmer concentrating on their stroke and neglecting breathing. Extreme effort. Lack of knowledge	Return to early stages of confidence building. Gradually build up breathing progressions. Constant practice
2 Wrong point of breathing in the stroke cycle	Lack of understanding. Incorrect arm action or weak leg action	Revise and build up efficient leg and arm actions so that breathing fits in rhythmically
3 Not breathing sufficiently	Fear. Rushing breathing phase. Lack of knowledge	Return to the progression for breathing in the relevant stroke cycle

Fault	Cause	Correction
Timing		
1 Lacking in flow (appears mechanical and fragmented)	Weak leg action. Incorrect arm technique – e.g. too deep a pull in back crawl	Return to *very* early part of the stroke and build up
2 Co-ordination of arms and legs incorrect	Weakness. Lack of understanding	Corrections as for 1

Breathing

Breathing does not necessarily come naturally in swimming: it is a technique that must be taught only in relation to a stroke cycle. Many pupils are afraid of putting their faces in the water; many more are completely ignorant about how and when to breathe in relation to the swimming strokes. Teachers and pupils must *understand breathing*, and then the tension will vanish.

EXHALATION AND INHALATION

Let us check that swimmers exhale firmly from the *diaphragm*. Too many choke in the water – the water enters the nose and mouth if they blow gently and shallow, i.e. from the throat. It is essential to teach *deep* breathing. Exhalation should be through the nose and mouth. Inhalation should be through the mouth, and a deep inbreath is important.

METHOD OF BREATHING

As already mentioned, there are two methods of breathing in swimming:

1 trickle breathing
2 explosive breathing.

Trickle breathing is the more leisurely method. Here, breath is exhaled through the nose and mouth over a *longer* phase of the stroke, and followed by *adequate* inhalation.

Explosive breathing is more dynamic and is used by the swimmer under pressure. Competitive swimmers automatically use this technique, and of course a beginner is also under pressure – they tend to be busy trying to survive! The latter forget to breathe and to hold the breath, and when they arrive at the side or 'parking point', they quickly exhale and gulp air in! In explosive breathing, air is *forced out* towards the end of the underwater arm sweep, i.e. when the major part of the sweep is over. This is followed by a *short* phase of inhalation when the air is gulped in after the mouth has cleared the water.

I recommend trickle breathing for its longer phase of exhalation and inhalation.

Once exhalation is mastered, inhalation follows automatically. There are *three* main points for the teacher to stress:

1 the point that exhalation and inhalation should relate to the *arm cycle* of the relevant stroke:

- *front crawl:* when the *right* hand enters the water until the *right* hand re-enters the water.
- *back crawl:* when the *right* hand enters the water until the *right* hand re-enters the water.
- *breaststroke:* when the arms extended in advance of the body in the glide phase *start* to pull until the arms return to the start of the pull again.
- *dolphin butterfly:* when both hands enter the water following the overwater arc recovery with the arms until the hands re-enter the water again.

2 *when* to open and close the mouth in relation to the water – it can be most distressing, in the front crawl for example, to inhale before the mouth has cleared the water!

3 The *angle* and *movement* of the head during breathing – i.e. does the head stay rock steady as in the back crawl, rotate sideways as in the front crawl, rotate sideways or lift forwards as in the dolphin butterfly, or lift forward as in the breaststroke?

NB: in the front crawl (as already mentioned) a swimmer breathing to one side is said to breathe *unilaterally*. Here, they can breathe to the one side each cycle or every alternate cycle, or hold the breath and breathe maybe every third or fourth cycle. This type of breathholding is often used so that the swimmer can concentrate on the rest of the stroke rhythm.

If the swimmer takes a breath to one side and the next breath to the other side, this is called *bilateral*. This usually occurs every 1½ cycles.

Breathholding is sometimes purposely used in the following situations:

- into the final few strokes approaching and coming out of a turn. This helps the swimmer to concentrate on the stroke rhythm, the stability of the body and the power of the arm pull.

- following a start – again to enable the swimmer to concentrate on the stroke rhythm, the stability of the body and the power of the arm pull.
- during the stroke cycle of the front crawl and the dolphin butterfly. In the front crawl, for example, they might breathe to the one side every other cycle, or in the dolphin butterfly breathe every other or every third cycle and so on. This is mainly to prevent too frequent disturbance of the body position during the swimming phase.
- in the front crawl, where bilateral breathing is a form of breathholding. The swimmer breathes every 1½ cycles. This technique is used by teachers often to help body stability for an extra ½ cycle, and in a speed race to 'keep the eye' on other swimmers. In swimmers who have trained for years, it can help the wear and tear on the neck/shoulder. In a swim across the English Channel, swimmers train on the bilateral front crawl since, during the swim, they can then keep the pilot boat in view.

The other value in all strokes is that a certain amount of breathholding can aid buoyancy.

Early and late breathing – this is easier to understand if you consider when *exhalation commences* in the arm cycle for the stroke you are observing – for example, in the front crawl and back crawl trickle, you blow out as your breathing-side arm commences its underwater pull sweep. In contrast, if the pupil holds the breath until the last third of the arm propulsion, it becomes late breathing and is usually forced and explosive.

▶ TEACHING BREATHING

The front crawl

- Pupils should first choose their favourite side for breathing. They can be made to understand how their head rolls to one side in the water by getting them to stand in the shallow end, spaced out not directly beside another pupil, with their shoulders just under the water. They should lean forward, piked at the hip, with feet staggered, heels down and knees slightly bent for stability, with hands on the knees at this stage. Instruct them as follows: 'Imagine the nose is resting on a table, eyes looking downwards; roll your head to one side and rest your ear on the table. Repeat this numerous times and work towards a smooth rhythm and head roll' (rather like a chicken on a barbecue spit!).
- The non-breathing-side foot should now be moved forward and the breathing-side foot further back. Each pupil should hold up the hand which is on their breathing side and wave it at the teacher. This is their breathing hand. The other hand, the non-breathing-side hand, should be

glued to the non-breathing-side knee underwater. When the hand on the breathing side enters the water, the swimmer starts to exhale through the nose and mouth. The face is held steady as the swimmer exhales, pulling the arm through the water. As the arm passes under the nose, the head is rolled sideways, with exhalation continuing. The hand reaches the thigh, and the elbow lifts from the water. Exhalation should be completed when the mouth has cleared the water. Inhalation usually commences as the elbow clears the water in the arm recovery over the water. The head is returned during the arm recovery and must be in the starting position with the nose in the water ready for the arm cycle again.

- This breathing phase should be repeated every cycle.
- Once the breathing cycle has been mastered, bring in the other arm but continue to breathe in relation to the breathing hand. This takes place while still standing in the shallow end.

The pupil should then swim a few metres front crawl using arms and legs, with the face in the water holding the breath with the head steady. They need to think hard and to prepare to fit *one* breath at 2–3 metres so that the rhythm flows evenly – 'flow as you go!' If the pupil copes, add more breaths per 5–10 metres until the swimmer is breathing every stroke cycle.

The back crawl

Breathing is easy in this stroke as the face is clear of the water. It is usually fitted into every cycle, and is fairly automatic. Trickle breathing is preferable for the beginner. If the swimmer is not breathing, catch their eye, remind them to 'blow as you go' and visually demonstrate exhalation! I usually tell the pupils that it is very similar to the bellows of a fire or an accordion, i.e. as you squeeze, you blow out, and as you open, you breathe in.

You can again teach the breathing in relation to the arm cycle. It would simplify it for the pupil if you again say to them: 'Choose one arm and wave it at me' – that, again, is their favourite breathing arm. As the favourite arm enters the water in an extended position in advance of the head, exhalation through the nose and mouth commences, and is completed as that arm reaches the hip, and inhalation commences as the extended arm clears the water, drawing an arc over the surface. The mouth is shut, and the breathing cycle commences again.

The breaststroke

Although explosive breathing is used by competitive breaststroke swimmers, trickle breathing is more suitable for the beginner as it is comparatively easy to teach. Here, the face should be looking forwards and kept comparatively clear of the water. Inhalation takes place through the mouth as the arms sweep out and down. This movement lifts the body and is therefore ideal for the inbreath. The elbows tuck to the sides, and as this occurs, the mouth should be closed. As the arms extend forwards into a glide position, the legs usually kick back in a basic breaststroke. As the legs drive and the arms extend, it is easy to say 'Blow the hands forwards!'

The dolphin butterfly

Here, the swimmer can breathe forwards or to the side, but if side breathing is used, the swimmer must make sure the shoulders remain symmetrical. Side breathing can help to maintain a flatter body position, but forward breathing is more popular. Whichever position the swimmer chooses to breathe in, it must be timed correctly with the arm cycle and leg kick. A flexible neck is an advantage.

Breathing will be explosive and late in this stroke. The exhalation through the nose and mouth commences during the latter third of the underwater arm sweep as the hands are passing under the nose and travelling towards their hips. The *second beat* of the two-beat dolphin stroke coincides with the *start* of exhalation, and at this point the head is being raised. The short exhalation is completed as the mouth clears the water. Inhalation takes place at the beginning of the recovery. (The elbows are usually clearing the water at this point.) The mouth is shut during recovery, and the head is lowered and the face in the water as the arms re-enter the water following the low recovery.

Alternate breathing, i.e. breathing every other cycle, keeps the body flatter.

Starts and turns

▶ ## RACING STARTS FROM THE POOLSIDE OR STARTING BLOCK

Many pupils enjoy racing, and it is for this reason that racing starts and later pivot turns have been included here. Consider again the views on motivation and competition in Chapter 3.

With the exception of the backstroke, most starts are from the bathside. The depth of the breaststroke start is slightly deeper, and even the back-crawl start is deeper than it used to be. This is to facilitate the legal stroke laws now permitted by the Amateur Swimming Association, and to make use of the follow-up starts. In the back crawl, for example, a swimmer is now allowed to remain submerged, following a start, for a distance of not more than 15 metres. In the breaststroke a swimmer is permitted to execute one complete arm and leg cycle, and then, into the second arm stroke, the head must break the surface at that stage in the pull sweep *before* the elbows tuck to the side. Dolphin-butterfly swimmers usually refrain from a deeper start despite the fact that ASA law enables them to kick more than once underwater, because they are allowed one arm pull before surfacing, so it isn't an advantage to remain underwater kicking legs only.

There are three types of start from the poolside: the *wind-up* or *swimming start*, the *track* or *staggered start*, and the *grab start*.

The younger pupils should be taught a basic start initially, and then they can progress to the more advanced techniques later. We shall therefore consider just the first of these starts here.

The wind-up or swing start

Preparatory stance

The swimmers take up their positions at the *back* of the starting block, or, if the bathside is being used, they stand a few feet back from the edge of the pool. The swimmer looks ahead at the pool, and concentration should be fully on the race.

Ready stance

The starter says 'Take your marks', and the swimmer now moves forward to the front of the starting block or bathside. The ready position must be comfortable. The feet should be hip-width apart, heels down, toes curled over the bathside or starting block. The knees are bent in a stable, comfortable position to suit the individual. The swimmer leans forward, curving the back, and with the neck following the curve of the back, but the eyes look very slightly outwards, at a point about 10 metres up the pool. The arms are in an extended position slightly in front of the shoulders, with the palms of the hands facing back.

The starter waits until all swimmers are steady.

Take-off

The signal to go can be a pistol shot, a whistle, the word 'Go' or a klaxon (bleep). The swimmer springs into action on the signal.

1   The arms swing forwards slightly, and the toes automatically lift at this point. The arms then move outwards and swing backwards. The body weight is transferred to the heels of the feet as the arms swing backwards and the head is lowered slightly.

2   The arms swing downwards and forwards. The body weight is now on the balls of the feet, with the toes firmly gripping the side. The body is lowered slightly before moving forwards and travelling outwards. The forward swing of the arms coincides with the outward progress of the body.

3   The arms should be swung to an extended position just above the ears, with palms downwards and thumbs quite close together. The head lifts slightly. The legs and feet are close together and extended as they dive.

Flight

The body should look like an arrow. It is extended and streamlined in every possible way. The body is also angled slightly for entry – this angle will vary a little according to the stroke.

Entry

The body is still extended. The fingers enter the water first, palms downwards and arms stretched. The head is squeezed between the arms. The body should be held firmly on entry.

Follow-up

Each start should be followed up by a glide in a stretched position, and as soon as the speed decreases the stroke commences. Advise the pupils not to overkick in the front crawl before their arm action is under way: this can act as a brake to forward movement. Breathholding for the first few strokes in the front crawl and dolphin butterfly is usually an advantage as the swimmer can concentrate on getting the stroke rhythm going.

THE BACK-CRAWL START

The back-crawl start occurs *in the water* but can be considered under the same headings as those for the wind-up or swing start.

The preparatory stance

The swimmers in the water place their hands shoulder-width apart on the rail, in the trough, or on the bathside, or gripping the starting-block handles. The swimmer must face the wall and place the balls of the feet on it under the water surface. The feet should be apart, either on the same level or one foot a little higher than the other – this gives stability. The knees are in a tucked position; the body is compact but comfortable, with the arms extended as the hands grip the starting point. The eyes should look straight ahead at a point on the wall.

Ready stance

As soon as the swimmer hears the command 'Take your marks', they pull themselves closer to the wall by bending their elbows, curving their back a little more and tucking their chin in. The body is lifted right out of the water at this point. When all the competitors are still, the starting signal will be given.

Take-off

At the signal 'Go', the swimmer thrusts off the wall like a rocket by driving the balls of their feet hard into it. The knees are straightened and the feet extended. At the same time, the hands are released from the wall and the arms swing sideways and backwards over the surface to an extended position beyond the head. The head is uncurled from the tucked position and stretched backwards. The legs, arms, body and head *all* spring into action together on the signal, and co-ordination must be practised.

NB: it is important to check the hips are driven slightly upwards but mainly outwards at take-off.

Flight

The body is extended but slightly arched backwards in flight, with the arms and legs together and the feet stretched.

Entry

The hands should enter the water first. The body should enter the water at a slight angle so that the swimmer can glide underwater. The body should be extended, with the head tucked between the arms and slightly back. The depth at entry will depend on the follow-up the swimmer is using.

The follow-up

The swimmer will glide underwater in a stretched position, and in a very inexperienced pupil, when the glide returns to normal swimming speed, the legs should start kicking alternately. At the same time, *one* arm should start the underwater pull, leaving the other arm extended beyond the head, and then the stroke alternates in the normal way.

A more advanced swimmer should enter and go slightly deeper. As the glide speed slows, the arms should remain extended, with head between the arms and eyes looking upwards. The legs should move simultaneously, executing a dolphin kick on the back. The head must break the surface at 15 metres, and this can coincide with the arms breaking into the stroke rhythm – i.e. one arm starts the underwater pull, leaving the other extended beyond the head, and then the stroke alternates in the normal way.

TEACHING THE START

The front crawl, butterfly and breaststroke

1 The swimmer should be able to plunge-dive before learning a racing start from the bathside.

2 The plunge can develop with the emphasis on streamlining, shallow entry and glide.

3 Check the racing-start stance.

4 Make sure the depth of dive is right for the stroke being performed.

5 Work on picking up the stroke rhythm after the glide. This requires much practice.

6 The pupils should experience the various different starting signals and variations of the length of time between 'Take your marks' and 'Go'.

7 Push and glide work generally in the water from the bathside is valuable to provide the necessary feeling of extension at take-off, flight and entry. Breathholding for the few strokes following push and glide can also be introduced.

Back-crawl stroke

Follow the same progressions adapted to cover starting in the water.

For all *starts*

- the class can work lengthways, i.e. so many swimmers step forward on the bathside and start and swim up the pool in wave formation. The second rank steps forward, and so on. Or:

- the class can work widthways. They can all go at the same time or, starting at one end, go in one after the other down the line in the *cannon* formation.

Teaching points for starts

The front crawl, butterfly and breaststroke

The preparatory stance

Check the concentration of the swimmer. Upright stance, eyes forward on the course.

The ready stance

1 Feet positioned hip-width apart, and toes gripping the edge.

2 Knees bent for balance.

3 Back curved.

4 Neck following the curve of the back, but eyes looking slightly outwards.

5 Arms in an extended position, held in readiness for the swing.

6 Listen attentively for the signal to start, remembering that the length of time between 'Take your marks' and the signal to go may vary considerably. A good starter will vary the length of time to prevent any swimmer from gaining an advantage.

NB: the take-off can affect the flight considerably. Many swimmers pike during flight because they do not swing their arms far enough through on entry, or they aim their entry target at take-off a little too far out from the side.

The flight

Keep the body stretched and streamlined throughout. The body should look like an arrow, with feet and legs together and stretched; the arms can be extended and together, or extended and slightly apart.

The entry and follow-up

1 Keep stretched, and check that the angle is suitable for the stroke.
2 Time the commencement of the swimming stroke at the point where the speed drops to swimming speed. Avoid starting this first stroke too soon as this loses the advantage of a streamlined glide.
3 The swimmer may need to find the ideal depth to suit both their size and the stroke.
4 Check breathholding while getting into the stroke rhythm.

Teaching points for the back crawl

(Even though the start is in the water, ensure the water is deep enough.)

The preparatory stance

1 Check the concentration of the swimmer, eyes on the wall.
2 Feet slightly apart for stability under the surface.
3 Do not overtense at this point.

The ready stance

1 Listen for the 'Take your marks' signal.
2 Pull up closer to the wall on the signal – body curled and head tucked in slightly.

The take-off

1 The signal to 'Go' should cause a dynamic reaction from the swimmer. The drive should be hard.

2 The drive from the wall and swing-back of the arms should be coordinated.

3 The head should uncurl and help to lead the way.

The flight

1 The head is back and tucked between the extended arms.

2 The body should be slightly arched.

3 The arms should be as close together and as stretched out as possible.

4 The feet and legs should be together and stretched.

The entry and follow-up

1 The swimmer should remain stretched at entry, placing the head in an ideal position: not too far back as that would cause too deep an entry, or too tucked in as that would cause resistance.

2 The body must be at a sufficient depth to glide in an extended position underwater.

3 Carefully check that as the leg kick starts, *one* arm remains extended and *one* arm commences the semi-circular sweep to the thighs so that the stroke rhythm is immediately achieved. NB: many swimmers tend to pull both arms together and simultaneously to the side at this point and so delay getting into the stroke rhythm.

4 Swimmers with sinus problems may find the 'push offs' troublesome. They should *exhale* at this point and consider wearing a nose clip.

TURNING

Turns are vital to any swimmer, and can make a difference between winning and losing a race. Young children should be shown how to negotiate the wall as soon as they have developed their strokes sufficiently. I recommend a simple pivot for all strokes. As the swimmer progresses at a later stage they can learn tumble turns for the crawl strokes.

The following parts of the turn should be considered:

1 the approach;

2 the turn;

3 the drive-off;

4 the follow-up.

The *pivot turn* is a spinning movement with the body tucked up.

The front-crawl pivot turn

The freestyle swimmer is allowed to touch the end of the pool with any part of the body. A pivot turner will use their hands to touch it. (See Figure 10.2.)

The approach

1 The swimmer should approach the wall at full speed.

2 When the swimmer's head is approximately an arm's length away from the wall, the leading arm, e.g. the right arm, stretches out ready to touch the wall. The palm of the right hand should touch, with the fingertips pointing sideways, i.e. to the left. I usually say to children that it is their car indicator and that it points the way they wish to turn.

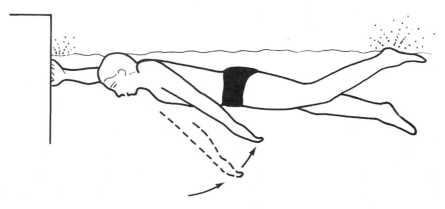

Figure 10.1 *Approaching the wall in the front-crawl pivot turn*

3 The left arm pushed back as in the normal front-crawl underwater stroke. The body at this point moves closer to the wall, and the right arm bends. The swimmer's head is now close to the wall, face in the water, eyes looking slightly forwards.

The turn

1 The body is tucked *tightly*, knees to the chest.

2 The left arm acts as a paddle, and is essential to aid the pivot. The palm of the left hand stretched out firmly, sweeps across the waist to the right side of the body. The body will be pivoting to the left. The right hand presses

hard into the wall and pushed out behind the right shoulder, completing the spin.

The drive-off

1 The body is a little lower in the water at this point, and tucked up. The arms are squeezed to the side of the body, palms downwards, hands to the side of the ears.

2 The feet are placed on the wall hip-width apart. The balls of the feet prepare for the drive.

The follow-up

The arms stretch forwards at the same time as the legs dive backwards. The body is now in a streamlined glide position. This position is held with the head tucked between the arms until the speed of the glide drops to swimming speed. The follow-up here is identical to the follow-up for the start.

The breaststroke and dolphin butterfly pivot turns

In the breaststroke, 'two hands must touch the wall simultaneously at, above, or below the water level. The shoulders shall remain in the horizontal plane until the touch has been made. The head may be submerged after the last arm prior to the touch, provided it breaks the surface of the water at some point during the last complete or incomplete cycle preceding the touch.'

In the dolphin butterfly, 'at each turn and at the finish the touch shall be made with both hands simultaneously, at, above or below the water surface. The shoulders shall remain in the horizontal plane until the touch is made.' (Amateur Swimming Association, 1997.) (See Figure 10.3)

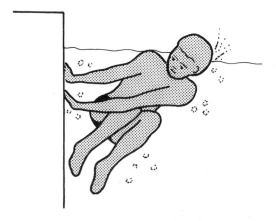

Figure 10.2 *The pivot turn for the breaststroke and dolphin butterfly*

In the breaststroke and dolphin butterfly, the follow-up for pivot turns is identical to the follow-up for the start.

The approach

1   The swimmer approaches the wall at full speed.
2   The touch is made with the body still on the front and with shoulders horizontal. Both hands touch simultaneously.
3   As the touch is made, the body tucks – I usually say to the children 'knees to chest and imagine you are sitting in a vertical barrel' – and the elbows are bent slightly.

The turn

1   The arms push away to one side, aiding the pivot – i.e. to the side opposite the direction of the turn.
2   The head is raised slightly, and the body sinks slightly.
3   The body is still tucked during the turn.
4   The opposite hand to that used for the pivot often sculls during the turn to aid balance and keep the body near the wall.

The drive-off

1   The feet are planted on the wall as for the front crawl.
2   A breath has been taken during the pivot, and the head is placed between the arms ready for the push-off.
3   The push-off is similar to the front-crawl, with the greater depth variations mentioned. The body must be on the breast at the push.

The follow-up

It is desirable to hold the breath for the first few strokes and pull strongly to get into the rhythm.

The back-crawl pivot turn

The body should be on the back at the touch, and should push off in this turn. (See Figure 10.1.)

The approach

1   The swimmer should approach the wall at full speed.
2   The leading arm, e.g. the left arm, is stretched back, and the palm of the hand touches the wall fingertips uppermost just under the water surface.

The right arm continues the underwater arm sweep as in a normal stroke. This helps the swimmer both to maintain body balance and to get closer to the wall.

3 The head is slightly *back* in the water.

Figure 10.3 *The tuck position in the back-crawl pivot turn*

The turn

1 The right arm is now sculling to aid a compact tuck and pushes firmly in a sweep to the *right*, enabling the tucked body to spin to the *left*.

2 The compact body should be lying slightly back, eyes up. (Say to the pupils: 'knees to chin, never chin to knees' – a common mistake causing the fault of turning onto the front.)

3 The tucked legs swing near the water surface to the side of the leading arm – i.e. the left side in this example. (I often tell the swimmers to imagine they are sitting on a plate and that they are to spin to one side or the other.)

4 The hands are then gathered near the head, palms up.

The drive-off

1 The body is still tucked. The feet are planted on the wall slightly apart, ready for the drive.

2 The arms are extended backwards, palms of the hands uppermost, as if the arms, head, seat and feet are pushing and gliding along a polished table top. Many pupils swing the arms out of the water at this stage, but they should instead keep their arms in the water.

3 The legs and body stretch at the same time as the arms extend.

4 The body is now in a streamlined position, gliding away from the wall.

The follow-up

The follow-up after the glide is identical to the follow-up after the start.

Marker flags are used in backstroke competitions to warn the swimmers when they are near the wall for their turn. Teachers can guide pupils in this respect by getting them to swim set distances and count their strokes. Eventually, they will know by the stroke count when they must prepare for the turn.

Teaching the turns

The class should be spaced out several yards from the wall. There are several suggestions for pool layout for turn practice: the class can work widthways or lengthways (see Figure 10.4).

Finishing

It is important for the pupils to practise touching the wall correctly at the finish of their swim:

- *front crawl:* 'Some part of the swimmer must touch the wall upon completion of each length and at the finish.'
- *back crawl:* 'When executing a turn there must be a touch of the wall with some part of the swimmer's body.' 'Upon the finish of the race the swimmer must touch the wall while on the back.'
- *breaststroke:* 'At each turn and at the finish the touch shall be made with both hands simultaneously at, above, or below water level. The shoulders shall remain in the horizontal plane until the touch has been made.'
- *dolphin butterfly:* 'At each turn and at the finish of the race, the touch shall be made with both hands simultaneously, at, above or below the water surface. The shoulders shall remain in the horizontal plane until the touch is made.' (Amateur Swimming Association, 1997)

Useful information

In *medley swimming* the children can eventually experience swimming all four swimming strokes.

- The order of swimming *individually* is: butterfly, backstroke, breaststroke, freestyle (freestyle means any stroke that has not already been swum, i.e. they cannot do butterfly, back crawl, breaststroke. Most swimmers choose the front crawl here as it is fast)
- the *team medley order* is: back crawl, breaststroke, butterfly, freestyle (the same rule applies for the freestyle swim as for the individual medley)

Individual work

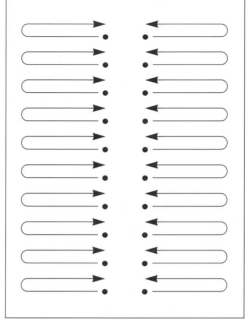

Pairs working back-to-back. An element of competition can be introduced

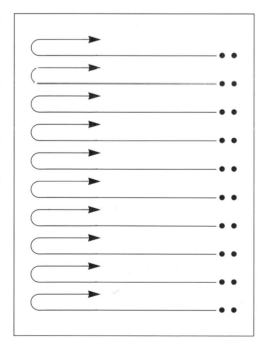

Pairs working alternately. Widths with turns can be timed

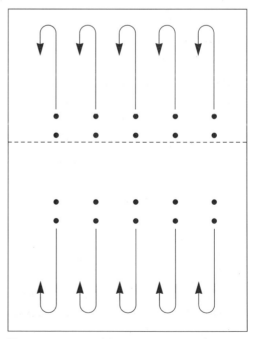

Two groups working on turns in alternate groups of five at each end

Figure 10.4 *Different pool layouts for turn practice*

Diving

Children love to enter the water head first, but before this is contemplated, the teacher must check the depth is adequate. Requirements will vary according to the type of dive and, to a certain extent, the heights of pupils. The Amateur Swimming Association recommends the following depths:

1 basic diving water skills in shallow water: no less than 0.9 metres;

2 surface dives in deep water: 1.5–2.0 metres minimum;

3 poolside activities (1.8 metres minimum, i.e. for stepping and jumps. Jumps should always be taken from standing take-off and related to the height and weight of the swimmer;

4 the plain header (see pages 118–120): minimum depth of water should be equal to the height of the diver with arms fully extended above the head plus 0.5 metres;

5 racing starts:

- from the deep end, a starting block up to 750 mm above water level may be used, pool depth 2.0–3.5 metres.

- from the shallow end, a starting block 500 mm above water level may be used, water depth 1.5–1.8 metres.

If diving is to be successful, the swimmer must be confident in water and be completely at home both underneath it and on the surface: if pupils are afraid of getting their faces wet they will not be happy diving. A good foundation of early confidence work is therefore necessary.

SHALLOW END ACTIVITIES

1 *Floating:*

- star shape

- tuck shape – similar to a mushroom float
- thin shape
- move from star shape to tuck shape to thin shape, in prone and supine positions, without putting the feet down. Roll over from back to front and repeat

2 *Picking objects up:* picking up bricks, discs, coloured pebbles from the bottom.

3 *Body weight on the pool bottom:* 'Which part of the body can you rest on the pool bottom?' 'Move and find another part – keep moving from one part to another.'

4 *Push and glide:* much confidence can be gained with the streamlining positions required in push and glide.

- Push and glide from the side into the prone position. Face in the water, head squeezed between the arms, body stretched. Stand up as the speed decreases.
- Push and glide and roll over in the longitudinal axis from prone to supine.
- Push and glide, tuck, stretch, stand up.
- Push and glide into a front tucked somersault and stand up.
- Push and glide into a front piked somersault and stand up.
- Push and glide underwater, raise fingertips and rise to the surface.

5 *Swimming through and under objects:*

- swimming through hoops.
- swimming under ropes.

6 *Springing activities:*

- in water of about one metre in depth, stand with feet apart one in front of the other and do handstands on the pool bottom.
- From a crouched position, spring from feet to hands as in a bunny jump. Work on the spring from the pool bottom.
- Stand a little more erect as in a crouch dive, with arms extended in a position as for a plain header. Give a gentle push from the pool bottom and land on hands. (Repeat this several times.)

7 *Jumping in:*

- standing jumps from the bathside; the knees must 'give' slightly as the feet touch the bottom.
- jumps from a short run, i.e. a couple of steps. Simple diving skills from the bathside can now be introduced.

THE SITTING DIVE

Sit on the bathside with the heels in the trough or on the rail a few centimetres apart. Extend the arms above the head with thumbs locked and the ears squeezed between the arms. Curve the back and roll gently forwards to overbalance so that the body rotates into the water. A useful teaching point is: 'Touch your knees with your nose as you lean forwards and then push outwards.' The top of the head should meet the water. (Many pupils who are afraid of water lift their head, which ruins the dive.) The water must be completely clear, and when the pupils come to the surface they should swim out of the way of other divers. They can practise surfacing by turning the fingertips upwards. Then, pupils can enter the water in a cannon formation, i.e. one after the other from the bathside, so that the teacher can see each dive. (See Figure 11.1.)

THE KNEELING DIVE

The pupil places one knee on the bathside and curls the toes of the other leg over the edge. The foot and knee should be side by side. The arms are extended, ears squeezed as for the sitting dive. Lean forward, with shoulders passing the knees, and keep the head down for a head-first entry. (See Figure 11.1.)

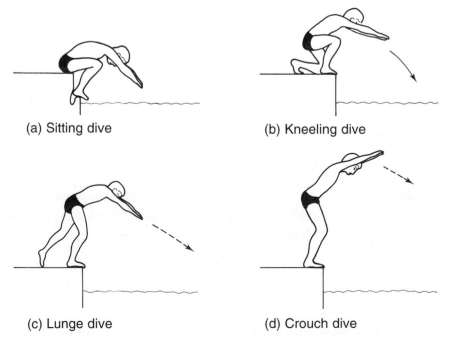

(a) Sitting dive

(b) Kneeling dive

(c) Lunge dive

(d) Crouch dive

Figure 11.1 *The sitting, kneeling, lunge and crouch dives*

THE LUNGE DIVE

One foot is placed on the edge of the pool, with toes curled over the edge. The knee is bent. The other leg is placed further back – the distance will vary between individuals – with the ball of the foot on the ground. The arms are in the same extended position as for the sitting and kneeling dive, with head squeezed between arms.

The pupil 'rocks' the weight of the body forward onto the front foot. The back leg is lifted, and the body overbalances and falls forward. The front leg pushes and lifts to join the other leg so that the body enters the water diagonally with arms and legs together.

The pupil should aim to bring the entry point a little nearer by pushing *up* more through the hips. (See Figure 11.1.)

THE CROUCH DIVE

Both feet are placed on the bathside about 15 cm apart, with the toes curled over the edge. In the early stages, the knees will be very bent so that the body is compact, and as the pupil becomes more confident the knee bend decreases. The back is curved and the head is squeezed between the arms which are extended and together.

The pupils should overbalance and drive from the feet somewhat outwards. The push becomes a more upward drive as the diver improves. (See Figure 11.1.)

THE PLUNGE DIVE

The *plunge dive* (see Figure 11.2) is required by front-crawl, breaststroke and dolphin-butterfly swimmers when starting from the bathside. It is also a useful lead-up to the plain header.

(a)   (b)   (c)

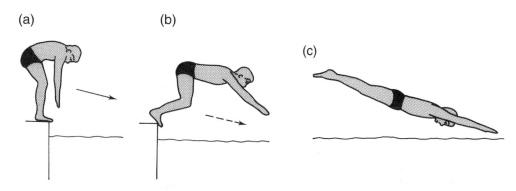

Figure 11.2 *The plunge dive*

The pupil places the feet hip-width apart, with toes curled over the edge and knees bent for stability. The back is curved, with the neck following the curve of the back. The arms hang downwards by the side of the body.

The arms swing back slightly, and the body weight is transferred to the balls of the feet. As the body falls forward, the arms swing forward to an extended position and the legs drive back. The body is now in flight in a stretched position. The entry is several feet from the bathside, and the angle is approximately twenty degrees to the water surface. It is important to streamline the hands at entry. The hands should be together, palms down, and the neck still in line with the body and between the outstretched arms. The legs and feet are together and also stretched.

Hold a streamlined glide position after entry. The glide can be maintained by keeping the body stretched, with the head between the arms looking downwards. When the swimmer wishes to surface, the hands can be tilted upwards and the head raised. The pupils will find the plunge dive invaluable both as a progression in learning to dive in head first and, when adapted slightly, as a racing dive.

THE PLAIN HEADER

The *plain header* is a more vertical dive, and can be attempted when the pupils have progressed through the other dives mentioned. Check that depth is sufficient.

The ready or preparatory position

The pupil should stand on the bathside in an upright position, with feet together and toes curled over the edge. The weight of the body should be over the feet. The arms are raised to an extended position in line with the body to make a narrow 'Y' shape. The palms of the hands face forwards, and the eyes look at a point just above eye level at the opposite side or end of the pool. The whole stance is firm and controlled.

The take-off

The body weight is transferred to the balls of the feet. The centre of gravity has been consequently altered, and the heels should be raised to help stability, with the knees bending slightly. The toes of the feet should now be gripping the edge firmly. The knees at this stage are straightened, and the feet drive upwards, extending as they do so; the push-up should be through the hips. The shoulders move slightly forwards, and the trunk bends slightly at the hips. The hips should remain vertically above the feet. The arms still maintain the extended 'Y' position, and are held in line with the trunk.

Flight

The feet have driven from the bathside or diving board at the beginning of flight, and the hips are slightly bent. This hip position is maintained during flight. The rest of the body is stretched. The arms are in the 'Y' position, with the legs and feet extended and together.

Just before entry, the arms come together, the hands are placed side by side and the head is squeezed between the extended arms.

Entry

The entry should be as vertical as possible. The angle of entry is governed by the angle of the diver at take-off and the height of the dive.

The body remains stretched until the feet have submerged.

Teaching points for the plain header

Ready or preparatory position

1 Feet together, toes curled over the bathside.
2 Posture controlled and body erect.
3 Head in line with the body, eyes looking forwards.
4 The arms in an extended position, palms of the hands face forward.

Take-off

1 Eyes still forward.
2 Body weight is transferred to the balls of the feet.
3 Knees bend and then extend.
4 Hips bend slightly.
5 Arms maintain the 'Y' position and remain in line with the trunk.

Flight

1 The body at the beginning of flight is slightly bent at the hips.
2 The rest of the body is stretched, with legs and feet extended and together.
3 The arms are kept in the 'Y' position until just before entry when they should be brought together and the head squeezed between the arms.

Entry

1 The body is as near as vertical as possible.

2 The hips straighten as the hands enter the water.

3 The body is stretched, and remains in this position until the feet have submerged.

Water safety

The National Curriculum states that water safety should be addressed at every key stage. The principles of water safety should be included and applied in every scheme of work.

Five to eleven year olds at Key Stages 1 and 2 should be made aware of the potential dangers of water in the home, at the swimming pool and in open water.

Throughout Key Stages 1 and 2 pupils should also be taught a code of conduct for visits to the swimming pool which covers safety, hygiene and discipline:

SAFETY AND DISCIPLINE

1 No swimmer should enter the pool until the teacher has given permission.

2 Swimmers should be aware of water depth and understand diving precautions. For example, a vertical dive from the bathside should not be made into less than 2.6 metres of water. The diver should look before diving to make sure the area is clear of other people.

3 On no account push others into the pool.

4 No running on the poolside.

5 Respond promptly to signals. A whistle or siren can be used in dangerous situations, but the children must know exactly what the signal means and what to do in emergencies. When a whistle is blown, all activity stops immediately, and attention is focused on the teacher. (In normal teaching, the use of a whistle, which has a violent, aggressive tone, creates an adverse atmosphere in an enjoyable working environment and so should be avoided except in exceptional circumstances.)

6   No pupil should swim immediately after a heavy meal, and they should understand why not.

7   Rope should be used to mark off safe areas for pupils of different abilities. Curlene rope (rope especially made to stand up to wear and tear in chlorinated water) is useful for marking safe areas of the pool. Coloured cork and buoys tied to the rope are also valuable. Groups and pupils should know where their boundaries are.

8   No pupil should chew gum in the swimming pool. This is highly dangerous.

9   Pupils should know how to help themselves if they get cramp. They should be instructed to use the unaffected limbs and to get to the side where help is usually available. They should also know what to do if help is not available.

10 Pupils should know where to obtain first-aid equipment.

11 Pupils should not wear jewellery of any description in the pool.

12 Non-swimmers should wear coloured caps to identify them. This is a particularly important consideration for teachers working in open water. Red, yellow, luminous pink, orange etc. are all good. Different-colour caps can be worn by different ability groups.

13 In a public pool, there must be strong swimmers or lifeguards to keep watch over the group.

14 Long poles and life belts should be placed at set points and pupils instructed in their use.

15 The teacher must have a sound working knowledge of methods of resuscitation. The teacher must also be able to swim competently and if necessary rescue and land any pupil in their charge.

Important: all teachers of swimming must have a copy of *The Royal Life Saving Society Handbook* and know it well.

HYGIENE

1   No one should be allowed to wear outdoor shoes on the poolside.

2   Pupils should not swim if they have any foot or skin infection.

3   Pupils should not swim if they have a heavy cold or an ear problem.

4   Pupils should use the toilet and the shower before getting into the pool.

5   Any pupil who has long hair should wear a swim cap. This promotes hygiene and swimming efficiency.

6   Swimming costumes should be rinsed out after use (but *not* in the pool).

7 For normal swimming lessons, pupils should only use goggles if there is a medical reason.

THE WATER SAFETY CODE

However, this is just the beginning: all pupils must also be familiar with the Water Safety Code. This has been devised by the Royal Life Saving Society (RLSS) UK and endorsed by the ASA.

1 Spot the dangers – learn to avoid hazards.

2 Take safety advice – for your own benefit.

3 Don't go it alone – loners live dangerously.

4 Learn how to help – yourself initially, and then others.

Drowning is usually the result of misjudging the situation and one's own swimming ability.

Pupils must learn and understand the Water Safety Code and be able to apply it to:

- home and garden
- swimming pool
- lakes, rivers, streams, reservoirs, ponds and canals
- parks and boating lakes
- the local environment
- the beach
- farms and the countryside

It is important for pupils to be able to apply the Water Safety Code not only to various locations but also to the activities that may be carried out in those locations – e.g. sailing, fishing, surfing, water skiing.

Pupils initially need to understand the rules of water safety. The theory of water safety can be taught as a stand-alone subject, but it must be balanced with the practical skills needed to cope with a wide variety of situations. Pupils need to develop their own swimming ability and to be able to swim in a variety of conditions. It's one thing to be able to swim in a warm, calm swimming pool, but open, very cold water presents a very different situation. Pupils need to have an awareness of the dangers of cold water, *hypothermia* (an abnormally low body temperature resulting from exposure to cold weather), and the effects of wearing clothing (unless clothing adds to the danger – i.e. through waterlogging and becoming very heavy – it should be kept on to keep the body warm). Pupils need to be confident in a wide range of swimming and survival skills. Practice in straightforward rescue skills should also be given –

i.e. throwing and reaching rescues. Care and commonsense need to be used both to maintain personal safety and, if the situation demands it, to help someone else. Pupils must understand the risks they face if they enter water to help someone else. In particular, a policy of 'Reach, throw, *do not go*' should be adopted.

In addition to learning about water conditions, hazards etc., pupils can also learn, at Key Stage 2:

- reaching rescues
  - using a pole (rigid)
  - using a towel or T-shirt (non-rigid)
  - using a rope
- throwing rescues – ball, float, lifebuoy etc. when learning to effect a throwing rescue, pupils must practise to improve throwing accuracy and then to increase throwing distance.
- *entries* from a height or lower level into unknown water.
- *swimming away* from the danger area – e.g. to clear a danger area where the swimmer might get hit by falling debris etc.
- *treading water* using one of four kicks:
  - breaststroke
  - cycling
  - flutter
  - egg beater.
- *floating*, which enables the swimmer to save a certain amount of energy and assess the situation.
- *surface diving*
  - head first and feet first
  - to avoid floating objects, or
  - to pick objects up underwater.
- *swimming strokes* where limbs are kept in the water, helping to conserve more energy than is the case with an overwater recovery – e.g. breaststroke, side stroke, inverted breaststroke on the back and sculling, and dog paddle. In an emergency, the swimmer should not swim unless forced to do so in order to avoid danger.
- *the help position* – the heat-escape – lessening posture.
- *the huddle position* – more than one person creates a close-knit group to help to retain body heat.
- *clothing* – non-restricting clothing that is not waterlogged or endangering life should not be removed hastily in an aquatic emergency.
- *exit* – the exit is as important as the entry, as assistance is not always available.

- *sequence* – combining the many skills in a survivor situation.
    - in open water, to prevent further cooling, turn on your back.
    - try to keep the head above water as long as possible: heat loss is greater if the head is occasionally submerged.

ENTRIES

For entries, the depth and area ahead of the swimmer should be suitable/adequate.

Explain to the pupils that in an unknown situation the swimmer may not know how deep the water is or whether there are dangerous objects in it, and that entries should therefore be shallow and feet first. In an emergency, any entry can be risky.

Slide-in entry

This is for when the depth of the water and the state of the bottom are unknown.

1 Establish a firm body, sitting with feet in the water.
2 Cover the body gently, taking the weight off the hands.

Step-In entry

This is for when the water is clear and the depth is known to be safe, and where the bottom is free from obstacles.

1 Look at the entry point.
2 Step gently off the edge. The knees are bent slightly, ready to give as the feet touch the bottom.

Tuck jump

1 Stand, with arms extended above head.
2 Take off, and tuck knees into chest.
3 Enter the water arms by the sides.

Straddle jump

This is for when entry is from a low height into unknown deep water. It is not to be used from a height above 1 metre or into unknown or shallow water.

1 On the poolside, one foot grips the edge and the other is placed back from the side.

2 Take off, with eyes looking forward, knees slightly bent. Aim for distance.

3 The top half of the body leans slightly forward, and the chest is well out.

4 The arms are lifted to shoulder level, sideways and slightly forwards and with palms down, and the elbows are bent. Hold the head still.

5 Some swimmers scissor-kick on entry to create resistance, thus keeping themselves at a shallow level. Press the arm down on entry. Keep the head above the water.

The compact-jump entry

This is from a height over 1 metre into unknown deep water. One arm pinions the other safely to the chest, with the hand of the latter covering the mouth and nose. Step off, with one foot leading. Then, bring the legs together, with a straight, vertical, streamlined body. Once underwater, tuck or pike to slow descent.

Treading water and floating

Treading water and floating enable a swimmer both to save a certain amount of energy and to assess the situation.

1 The swimmer remains on the spot, in a vertical position and with the head just clear of the water.

2 Sculling with the arms is carried out at the water surface. The arm movement is not unlike smoothing sand down on the top of a table, with the arms moving alternately towards and away from one another.

3 For the leg movements, the swimmer should select one from the following:

- the breaststroke leg action: the hands, flat, scull at the surface and the legs kick down in breaststroke style underwater;
- the flutter or front-crawl leg kick whilst the body is vertical; a flat scull at the surface, and the legs swing from the hips like a pendulum underwater;
- cycling: the hands, flat, scull at the surface, and the legs carry out a cycling type movement underwater.
- the egg beater. This kick exerts an alternate downward pressure which is continuous. The legs are bent so that the thighs are at an angle of 90 degrees to the trunk. The knees are wider than hip-width apart. The lower parts of the legs are responsible for the alternating cycling movement, with the knees maintaining the same level throughout. The

lower part of the left leg circles anti-clockwise and the lower part of the right leg clockwise, or vice versa. This movement is similar to sitting on a table with the thighs resting on the top and the lower parts of the legs moving alternately. To start the kick, the left leg is held almost parallel to the pool bottom with the foot dorsiflexed (bent upwards or flattened) so that it is 90 degrees to the shin. The right leg adopts an identical position to the left and begins to circle. The hands, flat, scull at the surface. Pressure should be continuous.

Surface diving

The swimmer may face danger on or under the surface. Submerging the head or the feet first should be taught:

1 *Head first* – used in known conditions:

- swim the breaststroke to the desired spot at a good pace
- look down into the water
- extend the arms to an underwater position in advance of the body
- make a strong breaststroke arm pull to the surface
- pike the hips into an inverted L shape, the head in line with the trunk and legs extended
- the legs and feet should be together, and the arms now by the hips
- turn the palms downwards and then press the arms downwards to an extended position in line with the head. The legs, held together, are lifted to vertical as the hands rotate and the palms and arms press down.
- submerge the head first in a vertical and extended position
- tuck the body, rotate onto front and swim underwater

2 *Feet first* – used if underwater area is unknown:

- swim the breaststroke at a good pace to the desired spot
- tuck from the prone to the head-up position
- make a strong downward breaststroke kick, coordinated with reaching both arms out of the water. As a result of the kick, the body rises
- The body sinks. Maintain the vertical position, with the arms extended. When an adequate depth has been reached, the swimmer tucks, taking the *seat* to the feet and keeping the trunk still vertical and the arms extended above the head. Then, rotate onto the front and swim forwards under water. (Keep the nose down and use large breaststroke arm and leg movements. The dog paddle can be used for variety.)

A good alternative is to keep the arms by the side of the body at the beginning of this surface dive. Turn the hands and palms uppermost and sweep the extended arms upwards against the water. This is a most effective movement in causing the body to submerge rapidly in the vertical position.

The help position – plus lifejacket

This is for when you cannot swim to safety.

- Float on the back
- Arms tucked and close to the chest, head kept out of the water
- Legs together and held diagonally down in the water

The huddle position – plus lifejacket

This is for more than one person. A close supporting position is adopted for one another to help retain body heat. The swimmers press the sides of their chests and their groins and lower bodies together, and part of the arms around each others' backs at waist level.

Exit

In the swimming pool, pupils can place their hands on the poolside, and, using a breaststroke kick downwards, press the hands down on the poolside. The body should rise, enabling the swimmer to pull themselves up on the side. A further kick, coordinated with a downward press, will allow the swimmer to climb out.

Sequence

The skills learnt can now be combined. If you have sole use of the pool, it can be more realistic if you divide the pupils into twos. One completes a circuit of skills and the other creates water waves making the water rough and more difficult to swim through. A battery-operated cassette player and a cassette with storm sounds – e.g. wind, rain, and thunder and lightning – from a 'sound effects' record add to the drama for the swimmers.

Lesson planning, organisation and evaluation

The details of the Programme of Study and Areas of Activity in the National Curriculum have led the PE teacher to adopt the pattern of teaching a six-week block of work on one activity and then to move on to another. In some instances, this has meant that the pupils have waited a whole year before returning to the first activity. Consideration of learning theories should lead the teacher to recognise that this is not an ideal pattern: by the time an activity is revisited, performance will have regressed almost to the start of learning. For physical skills to develop, there must be regular practice, and ideally, pupils should have daily physical activity at the primary stage. Where this is impossible, two shorter periods a week is more beneficial than one long session.

Whatever the pattern, an overall unit of work should be prepared, with aims, for the six-week or termly period. Out of this should flow individual lesson plans.

Each lesson should have aims or objectives, and the content of each lesson should be selected to fulfil these aims. A teaching-points column adjacent to the content should list the teaching points for each particular skill or technique. *Teaching points* are the information given to the pupils which will enable them to refine and improve performance. Alongside these two columns there should be a third which lists all the organisational aspects of the lesson. The organisation of pupils (in the pool and the changing rooms) and of equipment should be listed. If floats or other supports or aids are used, thought should be given to their storage and distribution. The greater the amount of thought given at the planning stage, the better will the lesson prove to be since more time can then be focused on pupil observation.

Following the lesson, an analysis or evaluation should be written. This should review the extent to which the aims for the lesson were fulfilled, and make observations on individual pupils' performances. It should be possible for another teacher, having read the evaluation, to then be able to take over the class. An indication of *why* aims were not achieved should be given.

LESSON PLANNING

Swimming in the National Curriculum at Key Stages 1 and 2, requires that each pupil show the following:

1   the ability to swim unaided, safely and with competence for at least 25 metres;

2   the development of water confidence, how to rest and how to adapt support positions;

3   various means of propulsion using legs or arms or a combination of both. The development of efficient and effective swimming strokes, prone and supine;

4   an understanding and practical application of skills for water safety and survival.

Planning ahead

The school swimming programme needs to be carefully planned, with economic and safety considerations worked out.

- Is a suitably qualified member of staff available from within the school, or does help need to be brought in from outside?
- Transport to and from the pool is another major factor. Is the pool within walking distance? Is it possible to share transport with another school?
- Timetabling also needs to be carefully considered, with adequate time allocated for travelling, getting changed and swimming.
- The number of sessions also needs consideration, as does the length of each session.
- The number of pupils in each session and their ability, in relation to the pool space and equipment which is available, also need to be considered.
- Are any extra helpers needed? If so, is there adequate insurance cover for them?

- Do any of the pupils concerned have medical problems, and if so, what provision needs to be made for these pupils?

Is the teacher in charge well qualified? In particular, are they:

- holders of a national body award?
- NVQ teachers of swimming?
- qualified teachers who have attended in-service training courses?
- holders of life-saving awards?

During the pre-planning period, a visit needs to be made to the pool and the following factors considered:

- the geography of the pool – shape, depth, width, length
- how many pools are available for use – learner pool, main pool
- first aid/safety. Emergency procedures. Telephone
- lifeguard cover
- the equipment available
- accessibility for disabled children
- the suitability of the changing area

Before the first lesson at the pool, a session in the classroom can be an advantage. Here, the pupils can be taught swimming pool conduct and safety and hygiene.

Cross-curricular links can also be made and used to great effect. For example:

- with science – buoyancy, resistance, propulsion
- with dance and drama – stretch, curl, glide etc.
- with mathematics – shape
- with environmental awareness – water safety
- with technology – design of equipment etc.

LESSON ORGANISATION

Initially, a beginners class can be taught as one group. Then, as individuals develop at different rates, the mixed-ability group begins to form. This can present a challenge to the teacher. The lesson needs to stimulate, challenge and be fun for the whole class. The three most important considerations are:

1 selecting appropriate material;
2 using the time and facilities available when planning the lesson;
3 organising the class to get the most from the lesson.

It is important that lessons be flowing and not fragmentary. The teacher who sets a number of widths to be swum will have a problem with the more able swimmers finishing before the less able. This creates gaps in the lesson and is boring for those pupils who are waiting around. It is better for pupils to work at their own level until the teacher commands the whole group to stop. One teaching point should be emphasised at a time, and the teacher can then move up and down the group helping individuals before moving on to the next point.

A demonstration by an able pupil will call a halt to the lesson but can be of enormous value. Here, the pupils need to get out of the water and stand on the poolside where they can see clearly. The teacher needs to focus the pupils on the relevant aspect of the demonstration, and then question the pupils to check their observation. It is then very important for the observing pupils to have a go themselves immediately after a demonstration has been shown.

Selection of suitable material

The following are the major considerations when selecting suitable material for lessons:

- the age of the pupils
- the ability of the pupils
- the lesson time available
- pool conditions – temperature etc.

When planning the lessons, the class organisation is also important. And again, the length, depth and width of the pool needs to be considered. The teacher needs to decide how best to section the pool off for the various groups – ropes should be used for this purpose.

Lesson layout

Lesson plans very considerably, but the aim is usually the same: the lesson should challenge, stimulate and be fun. Static sections of a lesson should be followed by very active ones so that a balance is achieved.

Lessons are usually set out in the following way:

1 *Introduction* – this should be planned to attract the attention of the class, get their interest and introduce the main part of the lesson. If the class seems apathetic or the water is cold, a lively introduction can work wonders. Sometimes, a demonstration can be used as an introduction, and

perhaps a verbal introduction may be appropriate. Whatever is used, it must stimulate.

2 *Main theme* – this is the main part of the lesson where new skills are taught or reinforced. Often the *whole–part–whole* method of teaching is used. In this method, the pupils first have an attempt at the whole stroke, giving the teacher a chance to assess them. Then the stroke is broken down into its component parts. Finally, the whole stroke is attempted again to see what improvement has been made.

3 *Conclusion* – this is a rounding-off of the lesson. It gives a chance for a demonstration by a successful pupil and a chance for everyone to have a final try.

4 *Contrasting activity* – this phase of the lesson gives the opportunity to introduce another aspect of swimming and can help to bring a lively end to the lesson.

LESSON EVALUATION

It is essential that teachers evaluate their lessons: think over what has been done and ask questions. The sort of questions that could be asked are set out under the following headings:

Teacher–pupil relationship

- Is the teacher confident, and do they have a good presence?
- Are the pupils at ease, attentive and do they have a good attitude to work?
- Are the teacher's requirements clearly presented and understood by the pupils?

Teacher appearance

- Is the teacher dressed appropriately for teaching swimming?

Teacher voice and positioning

- Is the voice effective in terms of height/depth, pitch, speed, enunciation?
- Can the pupils see the teacher when the latter is giving a teaching point?

Teacher demonstration

- Is this clear and accurate?

Preparation and planning

- Is the lesson content adequate for the level of the pupils?
- Is the work progressive, varied and well balanced?

Management

- Has due regard been given to safety and hygiene?
- Is the class well organised and under control?
- Is the available water space used to best advantage?
- Is there adequate flexibility in the class arrangement to allow group and individual teaching?
- Is the timing of the lesson satisfactory?

Observation and evaluation of pupils

- Does the teacher observe every pupil?
- Are the assessments of pupils' performances adequate?
- Is the teacher able to diagnose faults, find the cause and offer appropriate corrections?

Application of knowledge

- Does the teacher apply correct knowledge of swimming and use appropriate teaching points?
- Are the corrective practices suitable, and is the choice of progressive practices satisfactory?

General effectiveness

- Was the lesson successful?
- Did the pupils improve?
- Was the time in the water well spent?
- Was the lesson active, and did the pupils enjoy it?

Pool organisation

This will be affected by:

- teachers' knowledge of pupils – number in class, age, ability and type of activity
- knowledge of pool – length, depth, temperature
- equipment available
- whether the teacher is planning for a single lesson or a scheme of work

Beginners

An area of the pool which is an appropriate depth for beginners must be safely roped off. This available area can be used for exploring both at the surface and below water level. The activities tend not to be too formal, with the emphasis on experimenting with the tasks set. The teacher challenges the pupils both individually and as a group.

See the beginners lesson plan on page 137.

Improvers

Improvers can work widthways initially. Teachers should try not to set the numbers of widths to be swum.

(i)   Individually: across the pool and back.

(ii) In twos: individuals swim across and back, then twos take over.

(iii) In twos: individuals swim across and reach opposite side, then twos set off, and when they reach the opposite side, individuals come back etc.

(iv) In twos: individuals swim across, and when they reach halfway across, twos start off. When individuals arrive at the opposite side, they wait for twos to arrive, and then they set off again.

Once the class knows these patterns of working, the lesson will flow very well, and the teacher is free to move around to help give feedback and follow up comments to individuals.

In (ii), the amount of rest is predetermined. However, in (i), (iii) and (iv), the teacher will need to stop the children after a certain length of time. This rest time can be used to give feedback, ask questions, show demonstrations or set the next task.

A *pace clock* can also be used to set the amount of rest. The teacher can specify a period of time for the pupils to rest after a set number of widths.

Stroke deterioration, where this occurs, must also be the concern of the teacher.

Advanced swimmers

Advanced swimmers are more able to cope with increased distances and more challenging tasks.

Length swimming can be used as well as widths, and the pool can be partitioned off for either option, depending on the task set.

Rest (recovery) can be related to a partner or (as already mentioned) set by a pace clock. At an appropriate stage, a written schedule can be set by the teacher, allowing intensive practice for the pupil, freeing the teacher to work with those who need extra help. For example:

- legs only: 4 widths
- full stroke: 2 widths
- legs only: 4 widths
- after every one or two widths: 10 seconds' rest.

The pupils can swim in waves – see following diagrams.

Rest can be set by the teacher; or when the last one in the line arrives, the first one goes again; or again by the pace clock – 15 seconds at 25 metres, or 30 seconds at 50 metres.

Chain swimming

This is a demanding technique. The following factors need to be considered: age, speed, endurance, stroke.

See Figures 13.1 to 13.4 for various ideas of pool layout.

Pool organisation for various water activities

The diagrams illustrate some variations which might be utilised.

(a) Informal exploring pool area

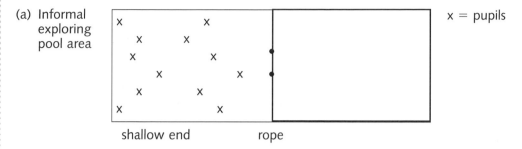

shallow end   rope

x = pupils

(b) Working widthways in learner type pool of constant depth

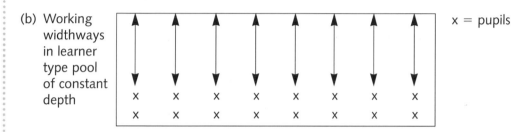

x = pupils

(c) Learner pool constant depth

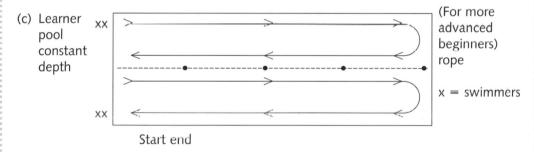

Start end

(For more advanced beginners) rope

x = swimmers

Beginners can do one length and, when the last swimmer arrives, set off back again or follow a mini chain system.

Figure 13.1 *Pool organisation and activities for beginners*

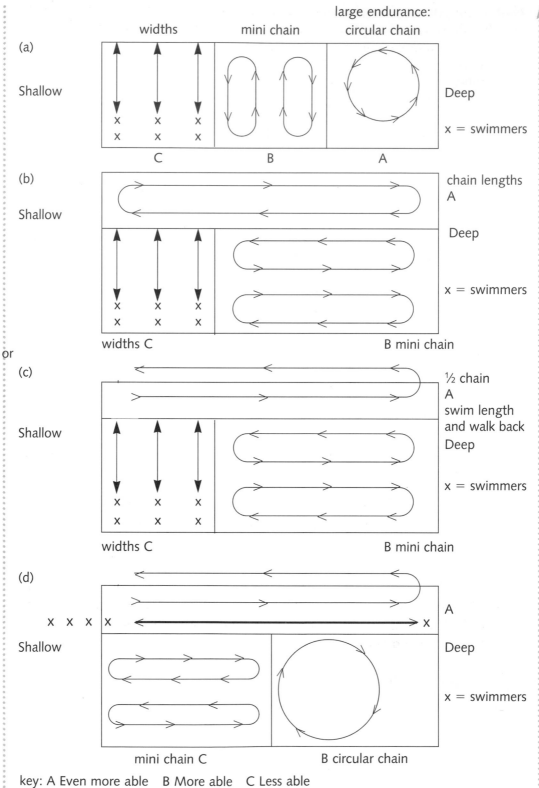

key: A Even more able   B More able   C Less able

Figure 13.2 *Pool organisation and activities for improvers and advanced improvers, and mixed ability*

Half of the group swims a length and then walks back. The other half swims a length, following the leader at 5-second intervals, and when the last one arrives, the first one swims back.

(a)

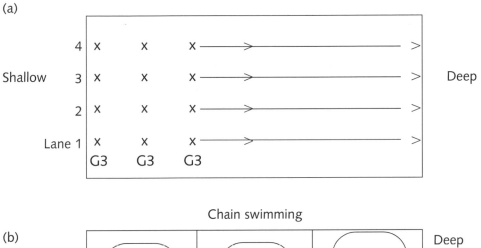

Chain swimming

(b)

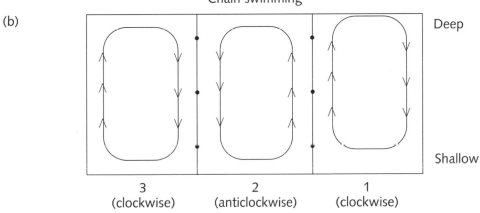

Figure 13.3 *Pool organisation and activities for advanced swimmers*

Group One (G1) swims from the shallow to the deep end, followed by Group Two (G2) and then Group Three (G3), at either a signal from the teacher or using a clock, leaving at 5-second intervals. They then return swimming in waves from the deep end.

Chain swimming

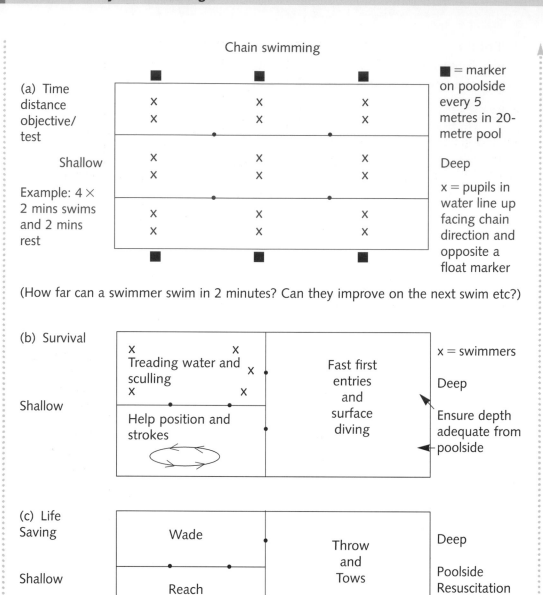

(a) Time distance objective/ test

Shallow

Example: 4 × 2 mins swims and 2 mins rest

■ = marker on poolside every 5 metres in 20-metre pool

Deep

x = pupils in water line up facing chain direction and opposite a float marker

(How far can a swimmer swim in 2 minutes? Can they improve on the next swim etc?)

(b) Survival

Shallow

Treading water and sculling

Help position and strokes

Fast first entries and surface diving

x = swimmers

Deep

Ensure depth adequate from poolside

(c) Life Saving

Shallow

Wade

Reach

Throw and Tows

Deep

Poolside Resuscitation

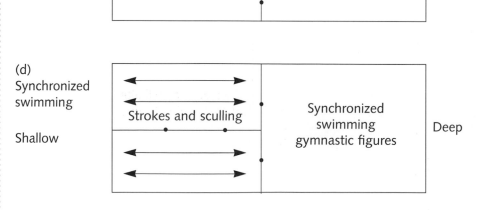

(d) Synchronized swimming

Shallow

Strokes and sculling

Synchronized swimming gymnastic figures

Deep

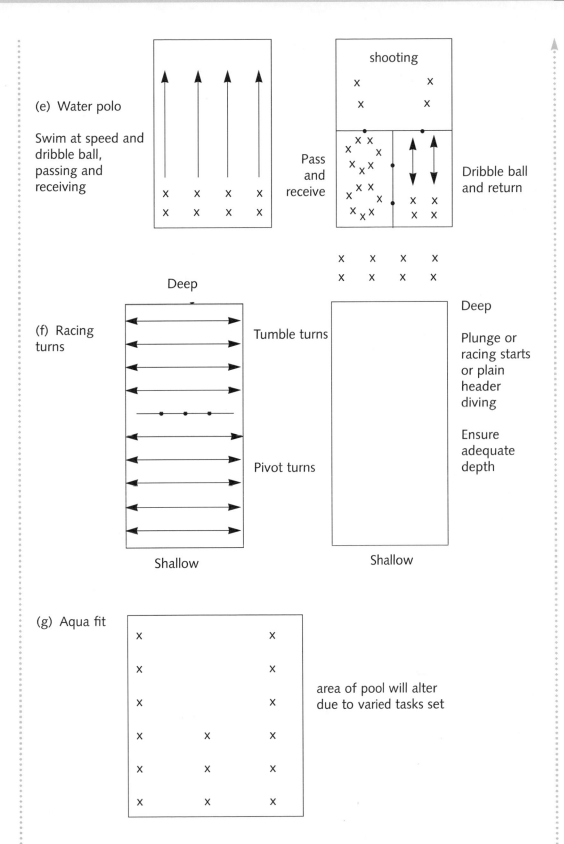

(e) Water polo

Swim at speed and dribble ball, passing and receiving

shooting

Pass and receive

Dribble ball and return

(f) Racing turns

Deep

Tumble turns

Pivot turns

Shallow

Deep

Plunge or racing starts or plain header diving

Ensure adequate depth

Shallow

(g) Aqua fit

area of pool will alter due to varied tasks set

Figure 13.4 *A variety of further activities for advanced swimmers*

SAMPLE LESSON PLANS

Example 1: beginners lesson

- Number of pupils: 20
- Length of lesson: 20 minutes
- Equipment: armbands; small balls; hoops; egg flips
- Previous knowledge: pupils have been introduced to water; they are non-swimmers

Aim: to develop water confidence

Material	Teaching points	Organisation
Either: (a) Entry via the steps	Face away from water Place feet on steps Hold on tightly Once feet touch bottom move away from side	Pupils in order or line
Or: (b) Entry via the side	Sit on side, feet and legs dangling over side Hands by their sides Move one hand across and place it by the other one Press down and swivel into the water	Pupils side by side on poolside
Movement		
Walking around the pool area, experiment with large and small steps	Walking, knees bent Shoulders in the water Arms wide to balance Small then large steps Place feet – heel then toe Lift feet by peeling off heel first Which of the above is easiest?	Limit area for activity Pupils spaced with no contact
Traffic Policeman Game	Travel in the direction the policeman points – forwards, backwards, sideways Face policeman all the time Keep shoulders underwater	Pupils facing policeman (teacher) spaced out

Material	Teaching points	Organisation
Floating		
Float on back – supine	Lie on back like a log Eyes look up Tummys up Feet up Make a long thin shape Make a star shape Stretch body	Pupils spaced out facing teacher
Float on front – prone	Roll onto front Keep arms in water Slide one arm across to meet the other, and roll over Make different shapes as before Look at bottom of pool	As above
Propulsion		
Prone – launching	Hold float at far end with straight arms Bend knees Keep shoulders in water Lean forward Push gently, lifting legs behind	Distribute floats from piles along poolside Start from poolside Move across width
Standing up	Lift head and shoulders Press down lightly on float Bend knees under chin to roll Hips below shoulders Stand up	Return to poolside
Front-crawl kick with float	Imagine wearing big floppy socks Kick them off Long legs Loose ankles Swing from hips Toes pointed Legs close together Small splash Blow as you go!	As above

Material	Teaching points	Organisation
Walking, blowing an egg flip	Chin in the water, blow hard Note what happens to egg flip	Within defined area No contact with others
Submerging		
Face-washing	Use nursery rhyme – 'This is the way we wash our face'	
Ring-a-ring-a-roses	Bob underwater on 'all fall down' Feet on bottom, bend knees, blow out, palms at side, turned out, press up, press bottom on to heels	In a circle, not touching
Watermanship		
Standard scull	Lie on backs Stretch body Eyes look at sky Tummy up Feet up Move using hands only Head first	

	Teacher demonstrates:
	    straight arms
	    fingers point up
	    hands firm
	    hands move like
	    windscreen wipers
	    wave at feet
		Teacher on poolside where all can see

	All try with steady rhythm;	Move across width of pool

Example 2: introduce butterfly leg kick

For a class of equal ability.

- Number of pupils: 20
- Length of lesson: 20 minutes

- Equipment: floats
- Previous knowledge: pupils can swim unaided and are water-confident. They have not attempted the butterfly stroke before.

Aim: to introduce pupils to the butterfly leg kick.

Material	Teaching points	Organisation
Introductory activity		
Push and glide prone	Hold rail or trough with both hands, shoulder-width apart Knees bent, both feet on wall Hard push off Body stretched Squeeze ears between arms Glide across pool as far as possible	Pupils in line at poolside Back to wall No. 1 behind No. 2
Main theme		
Push and glide underwater	Hold rail or trough Slide down wall Tip forward Push off Slide through water as far as possible	As above
Push and glide adding leg kick, underwater	Glide as before On slowing down, start to kick Keep legs together Kick up and down from hips Legs loose and relaxed Wriggle like a worm Use whole body like a dolphin	As above
As above, rolling from front to side, to back	Keep a steady rhythm	
Leg kick holding float	Chin on water surface Heels make small splash Points for kick as above	As above

Material	Teaching points	Organisation
Conclusion		
Leg kick at the surface, on the back	Teaching points as above Keep arms by the side	
Contrasting activity		
Jumping in, making different body shapes	Stand with toes over edge of pool Stand tall Eyes look forward Take off with 2 feet Jump up and out Make star, tucked, pencil shapes Return to normal vertical position before entry After entry, when feet touch pool bottom, bend knees and push back up to surface	Pupils swiftly out of water, in order Stand on poolside, in line, 1 behind 2

NB: teachers must check that pool depth is adequate for jumping in.

Example 3: front crawl

For a class of mixed ability.

- Number of pupils: 25
  - Group A: 12 Advanced swimmers
  - Group B: 9 Improvers
  - Group C: 4 Beginners
- Length of lesson: 20 minutes
- Equipment: armbands; floats
- Previous knowledge: all pupils have been introduced to the front crawl, but they vary in ability.

Aim: to improve the front-crawl stroke.

Material	Teaching points	Organisation
Introductory activity		
Pupils work widths on their favourite stroke A, B and C groups	Think about stroke rhythm Front and back crawl and butterfly aim for continuity Breaststroke, aiming for glide after each kick	Pupils swim at same time, if room; if not, 1 follows 2 Take breath when needed Keep going
Main theme		
C group:		
Leg kick holding float	Hold float at far end, arms straight Swing from hip Legs stretched Toes pointed Heels to surface, small splash Constant rhythm	In deep end of pool Swim widths Keep going Take breath when needed
Leg kick with arms extended	Thumbs locked Blow as you go Teaching points as above	
Dog paddle	Alternating arms Slide arm forward, catch hold of water, pull and push through to hips Keep kick going	
Front-crawl stroke, nose in water	Elbow leading recovery over water Hand close to ear as arm passes head Steady rhythm Breath held	
B group		
Dog paddle	Alternating arms Slide arm forward, catch hold of water, pull and push through to hips Keep kick going	In mid-depth Pupils start from side 1 follows 2
Full stroke, one breath halfway across	Keep rhythm uninterrupted Smooth roll of head, nose in water, ear in water	

Material	Teaching points	Organisation
Full stroke, 2 breaths taken across width	Teaching points as before	
Front crawl, breathing every stroke cycle	Work for a good rhythm	
A group		
Leg kick, arms extended	Teaching points as above	As above, in shallow end
Front crawl, breathing every other stroke cycle	Smooth roll of head Steady rhythm	
Front crawl, breathing to one side	Teaching points as above	
Front crawl, bilateral breathing (a breath taken on alternate sides, every one and a half stroke cycles)	Maintain a steady rhythm	

Conclusion
A, B and C groups: each group works on the last point once more

Contrasting activity

| A, B and C groups: Back tucked somersaults | Lie on back Tuck into very compact shape Bring knees up to touch nose Chin tucked in Arms sweep forward to make body roll backwards Stay near water surface | Pupils spaced out across pool, not touching |

Appendix I
Glossary of terms

Catch The point at the beginning of the propulsive phase where 'purchase' is made on the water. The hand 'fixes' on the water.

Dorsiflexed Toes pulled up towards the shins, i.e. in the breaststroke.

Downsweep The initial sweep used in the front- and back-crawl arm action.

Entry The point where the hand(s) enter the water after an over-water recovery, i.e. in the front crawl, back crawl and butterfly.

Explosive A type of breathing where forced exhalation (outbreath) takes place at the very end of the propulsive phase, and forced inhalation (inbreath) at the beginning of recovery. Breath is held in between.

Extension Stretching of a joint.

Flexion Bending of a joint.

Insweep The sweep which moves in towards the midline of the body.

In-toeing Where there is good ankle flexibility, the toes turn inwards towards the midline.

Limb track The path the arms follow during the propulsive phase of the strokes.

Outsweep The sweep outwards away from the midline of the body.

Pike The body is closed like an oyster shell. The arms and legs are extended and close together.

Pitch The angle that the hand is at as it sweeps.

Planar-flexed Pointed toes and stretched feet.

Prone Horizontal lying on the front.

Pull sweep and push sweep These refer to the propelling phase of the underwater arm action of the swimming strokes.

Push and glide As the arms release from the bathside, the elbows squeeze the ribs and slide forward until extended.

Recovery This is the phase in the arm action following the propulsive phase.

Streamlined Horizontal extension, with movements kept within body width and body depth.

Stroke counting Where the teacher asks pupils to count how many strokes they take for certain lengths or widths. If the stroke count increases too much – the pupil may be 'slipping' – i.e. a loss of 'hold' on the water. (A stroke cycle is from the commencement of a stroke's arm action until its recommencement.)

Supine Horizontal lying on the back.

Trickle A more leisurely type of breathing where air is exhaled and inhaled over a longer period.

Upsweep The sweep up towards the surface of the water.

Watermanship Total adaptation to various water skills on and under water.

Whip kick Used in the breaststroke. It is the more efficient propulsively of the two breaststroke kicks.

Appendix II
Analogies for the teacher of swimming

	Back crawl	Front crawl	Breaststroke	Dolphin
Body position	• eyes up • feet up • head: 'balance a pint of milk on forehead' • 'ears resting in water'	• 'eyes look for fish' • heels up • water cuts top of forehead	• head steady • shoulders square • balance a budgie on each shoulder • eyes look forward	• fish-like • like a dolphin • wriggle like a worm • eyes look forward underwater • like the man from Atlantis
Leg action	• kick a football, toes up • swing like a pendulum • toes brush past one another • long legs • use your feet like flippers • flipper feet	• heels up • swing like a pendulum • toes brush past one another • long legs • use your feet like flippers • flipper feet	• feet to seat • feet east and west • slow bend, fast kick	• legs together • flip like a fish tail • heels to surface like a propeller • equal rhythm

	Back crawl	Front crawl	Breaststroke	Dolphin
Arm action	straight & pull entry • arms enter like a knife through butter • hands on shelf • 'pinkie' first • close entry to head, 5 to & 5 past the hour	• in advance of the head • between nose and shoulder • firm hand, fingers together • elbow raised over a football	• arms stretched together like an arrow • shoulders square	• as for front crawl, but both arms together • shoulders square
	Catch: • Hold firm, imagine you are swimming through treacle	Catch: • Hold firm, imagine you are swimming through treacle • Get hold of a goldfish & put it in a box behind you • Reach out & touch the end of a long Alsatian dog's nose	Catch: • Hold firm, imagine you are swimming through treacle	Catch: • Hold firm, imagine you are swimming through treacle

Back crawl	Front crawl	Breaststroke	Dolphin
Propelling sweep: • straight arm • sweep dishes off a table, one foot under the water • thumb knuckle up	Propelling sweep: • thumb knuckle up • draw a line under the middle of the body • thumb to thigh, reach into your pocket	Propelling sweep: • elbows up, pegged on the washing line, sweep the inside of the mixing bowl • squeeze ribs • tuck arms to side	Propelling sweep: • elbows high, draw a keyhole with fingertips • thumb to thigh, reach into your pocket
s pull: • hold a rope, pull on it & push it • fingertips up • at end, press down to lift body as other arm enters			
Recovery: • thumb out • arms stretch like a blade • draw an arc over the water	Recovery: • elbows high • swing through a narrow pipe • touch ear with hand during over-water recovery	Recovery: • arms tuck, then stretch forward into narrow glide, slide just under water	Recovery: • elbows high, imagine a bird's wings clearing water with hands